Creating Spaces for Women in the Catholic Church

Edited by Sarah Kohles, OSF

Foreword by Teresa Maya, CCVI

Paulist Press
New York / Mahwah, NJ

Cover image: Fresco of a Christian Agape feast 2nd–4th century in the Greek chapel (Capella Greca) of the Catacomb di Priscilla in Rome. Courtesy Wikimedia Commons.
Cover design by Sharyn Banks
Book design by Lynn Else

Library of Congress Cataloging-in-Publication Data is available upon request

ISBN 978-0-8091-5628-3 (paperback)
ISBN 978-0-8091-8791-1 (e-book)

Published by Paulist Press
997 Macarthur Boulevard
Mahwah, New Jersey 07430
www.paulistpress.com

Printed and bound in the
United States of America

In gratitude for all those upon whose shoulders we stand,
especially for the women who support us and show us
how to carve out spaces for ourselves,
and for all those who struggle with the Catholic Church—
for those who stay and those who move on

CONTENTS

FOREWORD

I write this at the beginning of the Easter Season. I remain in awe of the community of women who went to the tomb one more time. They encourage me. These women must have been incredible because their story continues to reach us after two thousand years of patriarchy! Their witness must have been so powerful that despite centuries of sexism, we keep their memory. Nothing erased their names. I pray these women, apostles of the resurrection, bless and encourage the communities of women today who are inspired so deeply they are willing to "run back" to the places where our Church is still shackled by fear to tell a different story! This is my experience with this book.

In these pages, we are invited into the intimacy of the faith journey of vibrant, committed Catholic laywomen. They share stories, questions, sadness, and hope. What will we do next? Dismiss their witness like some apostles did, or "run to the tomb" like Peter? At the very least, we need to stay in their questions—ponder them deeply and allow them to move us to action. This much we owe each of these authors. They write with honesty and love for the Church as people of God. The authenticity of their voices challenges, prods, and encourages. After two years of pandemics, their reflections come to us when the loss of lives and livelihoods has challenged our entire human family, where uncertainty creates yet another pandemic of mental health; our anxiety betrays us despite our denial. What a refreshing remedy to read about the struggle to make meaning from committed young theologians. Lisa Cathelyn writes about the "pre-death waves of grief" that crash into the shores of your life. Like her, other authors are not afraid to share their grief, anger, frustration, or fear, permitting us to acknowledge our own experiences of them. This book takes us to "the tomb," to the places of grief and loss, to the places of discrimination and exclusion, and to the places of abuse, to learn there, with the first apostles of the resurrection, that God wants the Church to be where women belong and thrive!

The authors reveal a dimension of the mystery of the incarnation we must continue to explore: creation as the unfolding revelation of God's love for humanity. Each chapter challenges us to recognize the *imago Dei* of all people of God and how this influences how we theologize, live the liturgy, and practice every aspect of our faith. Their insights speak of table fellowship, kinship, and welcoming, and of the integration of mind, body, and soul—the mystery of God made human, who calls us to integrate, to connect, to welcome. They honor our humanity as God's creation, the experience of women as sacred. As Elaina Jo Polovick LeGault states in chapter 7 (perhaps the most beautiful description of the vocation of liturgist I have ever read): "Catholic liturgy holds the tension that Jesus was God and human." The Catholic community must embody this tension, embracing every aspect of our vulnerable humanity as God's loving embrace in the incarnation.

We need to claim their questions and stay with them. I am confident that you will be challenged by the questions, as each author grapples with the larger question of being a woman in the Catholic Church, "Why stay? Why go?" The focus is not "why we stay," Kristina Ortega shares but "how we stay." She offers a new question to pray with: How *do* we stay? The authors offer hard questions about the Church's challenged stance on sexuality and gender, the importance of inclusion and belonging of our Black Indigenous People of Color brothers and sisters, our ambivalence with queerness, and the entire LBGTQ+ community, and access to all forms of ministry in the Catholic Church. They also grapple with questions about what the abuse scandal does to the Church. With them, we need to ask many questions. What toxic cultures do we need to purge from our communities? What do we need to do so our Church is "not the abusive partner" to move away from, as Elaina so graphically describes? Which will sadly ring true to many readers.

The hope offered in these pages resulted from an authentic culture of encounter. The process that created this book should inspire other conversations, a table fellowship of women with a vision of the transformation our Church is called to. Each chapter is the result of meaningful conversations. We go forth with the challenge to create more spaces, to welcome new conversations with all who are willing to risk *Encuentro*! Collaboration affirmed each author's experience and gave her the courage to share a vision of theology in practice that can make a difference.

The conversations weave a powerful community, ready to usher in the emerging future. The authors compel us to engage in conversation with other women, with people committed to creating welcoming communities. We are also challenged to remember, to engage in a conversation with the women who came before us—the dangerous memory of those who struggled with a Church not ready to welcome their gifts and built the Church anyway. The authors created a space for conversations where they found their voice. We are invited to host, promote, and participate in our conversations, too.

This book calls us to be people who go forth, *gente en salida*, as other-centered people. Like many women before them, the authors found their voice in service and community. Many share stories of volunteer work, social activism, or their time in Catholic Worker as opportunities that deepened their spiritual commitment. Their faith journey is rooted in the prophetic task of justice. We find in them the energy of a new generation of theologians who understand that *lo cotidiano* (daily living) and the work of justice are sacred spaces for theologizing. I enjoy the analogies to the world of sports and business. Their spiritual growth, insight, and experience of the divine take place during the night shifts of hospital chaplaincy or getting the family ready to leave the house in the morning. They are all about creating kinship. The next generation of Catholic women activists will find echoes of their voice here. As the pillars of the post–Vatican II feminist struggle get older, they will find in these pages the torch has been passed. Their struggle is now in good hands. The words of the *Magnificat* come to mind: "from one generation to the next."

Reading *Creating Spaces* challenges us to include…All. Mary Perez reminds us that Catholic is always plural. No single cultural expression can embody the breadth and depth of our Catholic experience. North American Catholics can offer this gift if we can learn to embrace all the diversities in our Church, not just the ethnic and cultural diversities, but class and gender, and theological outlook. A polarized society needs the witness of a people of faith who cherish and live with diversity as God's Creation. We need to seize this time; we all deserve a Catholic Church where ALL are welcome, where ALL belong. The authors challenge us as a Church to be the community of belonging that welcomes and accompanies. Yet, welcoming needs work. Translating the core of our tradition into the language of inclusion will take intentional dedication. We need to go forth to continue this work. Stephanie Boccuzzi writes that "discovering feminist theology 'ruined' theology for me" because it created awareness of the lack of female voices in theology. A welcoming community notices who is missing around the table!

This book is not just for women. I pray many men also read it! We need men like Jesus, who created space for women in his ministry, who spoke and truly listened to women, praised them, welcomed them to discipleship, and sent them as apostles of the resurrection. We need to go forth and invite our fathers, brothers, friends, priests, and bishops into the kinship of God's holy people. Often in the stories recounted throughout the book, we learn of men who mocked or even assaulted and, just as sadly, who remained silent. The transformation the Church is called to needs women; if they continue to experience the deafening silence that makes them feel unwanted or unnecessary or doubt their gifts, they will have to move on to life-giving spaces. We need men, like Jesus, who dare to speak, ask questions, learn, include, and accompany. We should be encouraged because these men are also in these pages. Some are friends, husbands, and mentors who have journeyed with women. They have run with Peter to the tomb. They offer a glimpse of the Church we can become. They, too, are harbingers of the dawn that *will* come in the *Kairos* of God.

We are invited to this spiritual journey. Each of the authors ultimately shares from the heart of her faith. They dare to be vulnerable about their own experience of the divine. They name a spiritual journey, a lifelong commitment to listening for the whisperings of the Spirit. We need to claim this commitment to deepen our spiritual life and embrace the gift of our tradition available to all people of faith. As God's spirit deepens the roots, we will weather the storms ahead; we will be stronger together as a worshipping community. We will move from faith to action to be about justice. We will return to the theological task our time demands, making meaning out of our human experience in a time of breakdown, uncertainty, and vulnerability. We will do the work of transformation.

We are learning this journey is a synodal journey; we accompany one another, and no one should go alone. May these authors inspire other young people to create spaces for inclusion and conversation. May the number of voices increase to join others worldwide in India, Germany, or Chile. May this synodal pilgrimage gently but steadily include other voices who will participate, speak, write, and publish. May we keep asking questions because it should break our hearts to read, "In every space I entered, I wondered if I was truly welcome." A deep movement of the spirit has begun. I thank each of the authors for offering their story to this deeper story. We know the Church is in crisis and in the dark over its many scandals, experiencing death. Synodality is an invitation to move away from fear to risk the message of the empty tomb. We need a synodal pilgrimage to the promise of Easter. I treasure the questions these women offer because they give me hope. There is another way of being church. God is making something new. In their own words: "if we could only believe, there is the chance for new life and a moment for true creativity." What an exciting time to be a woman in the Church!

With Sarah K., Caroline, Silvana, Stephanie, Mary, Lisa, Kristina, Elaina, and Sarah, I wait for dawn and will go to the tomb. They are good company!

Sr. Teresa Maya, CCVI
Easter 2022

ACKNOWLEDGMENTS

This project owes much gratitude to Giving Voice and the Conrad N. Hilton Foundation. Giving Voice's witness to grassroots leadership and collaboration shaped this project. Giving Voice members' willingness to share their wisdom and resources with a collaborative effort between sisters and laywomen to create a space for exploring women's experiences in the Catholic Church has been a gift. Thank you to Giving Voice for sharing their grant from the Hilton Foundation to support these efforts, which allowed us to gather in person for a discernment retreat and a writing retreat. The ability to pray, ponder, and write together has been a tremendous gift and deepened our insights. Many thanks also to the Hilton Foundation for their ongoing generosity toward women religious, without which so much would not be possible.

Thank you to Stephanie Boccuzzi, who assisted in writing the first round of book proposals. Thank you to Amanda Kaminski for facilitating the discernment and writing retreats, as well as her endless encouragement of contributors. Thank you to Crystal Catalan, Teresa Carino, and Ana Lopez, for adding your voices to the retreats and the conversations we had around this important topic. A tremendous thank you to Caroline Read, who assisted me with the initial editing of these pages, and to Mary Perez—both served as sounding boards and offered their insights throughout the creation of this book. Thank you to Casey Stanton and Luke Hansen for creating beautiful and effective processes for assisting people in incarnating their dreams for the Church and world. Casey and Luke's Discern–Dream–Scheme workshop helped to refocus this project in the midst of the pandemic. Thank you to Teresa Maya, CCVI, for her personal example of faithfulness and challenge, as well as her insightful response.

I am especially grateful to all the laywomen and women religious who have been conversation partners in exploring soul-searching questions about living faithfully as women in the Catholic Church. As Paul says to the Philippians, "I thank my God every time I remember you" (Phil 1:3).

INTRODUCTION

Sarah Kohles, OSF

I remember the first time I experienced categorical dismissal because I am a woman in the Catholic Church. As an eager undergraduate studying theology, I was invited to a lunch with the chair of the theology department, a handful of other theology majors, and a priest who was considering setting up a scholarship at the college I attended. The priest asked questions throughout the lunch. I noticed that when most of us responded by discussing our coursework and pointing out the opportunities we had for internships at local parishes, the priest stared at his plate, looked around the school cafeteria, and ignored us. I was confused by his behavior. After all, he is the one who wanted to meet current theology students. However, when the one male student in our group chimed in and shared the very same information the rest of us had shared, the priest looked at him attentively, asked follow-up questions, and entered into an engaging conversation with him. The rest of us students—all women—may as well have been invisible and silent. Utterly shocked, I discovered there was no space for women at that table.

Sadly, my story is not unique. Many women struggle to find room to remain in the Catholic Church. Women are leaving the Church in higher numbers than men,[1] and more recent statistics indicate that, though many women remain, they are increasingly less involved.[2] Yet, women are searching for a way to stay and remain engaged with the Catholic Church they love, the Catholic Church that has preserved centuries of sacred wisdom. I have heard women ask soul-rending questions as they attempt to remain such as:

- How do I baptize my daughter in the Catholic Church? Look how they treat women! Look how they treat you, a sister.[3] It breaks my heart, but I just can't.
- We remain Catholic in the hopes that our granddaughters will know a different Church. Do you think the Church will ever recognize the gifts of women?
- I realized that remaining in the Church was like remaining in an abusive relationship. Am I unhealthy for wanting to stay in this relationship?

The words of these women haunt me. It is painful to watch the Church I love push so many faithful, gifted women out the door. I am left with many searching questions of my own: Does this have to be the way it is? Do we simply throw up our hands and admit that there's nothing left for women in the Catholic Church? How can we abandon the traditions and beliefs that have sustained us? How do we hold on? Is it possible to transform the Church from the inside? How might we actively create spaces for women in the Catholic Church? What if the key to transforming the Catholic Church is helping these questioning women to fully use their gifts? What if creating and claiming space allows women to find a reason to stay?

STATE OF WOMEN IN THE CATHOLIC CHURCH

How does anyone briefly summarize the experience of half of the population of Catholics in the world? Or even in the United States? This is an impossible task. All women do not have the same experience of the Catholic Church. The women who contributed to these pages have their own unique stories and perspectives based of the variety of identities they hold: race, ethnicity, gender, education, abilities, political affiliations. Yet, it is necessary to sketch the state of the Church for women.

Women have long played key roles in handing down the faith generation after generation. They find sustenance in the Sacred Scriptures, the sacraments, in Jesus, moral and ethical teaching, the long tradition of social justice, and the community of saints. Many of the ministries offered by our parishes are fulfilled by women: catechesis, the cleaning and upkeep of sanctuaries, hospitality at funerals, outreach to those in need. Women serve as youth ministers, directors of religious education, and even parish administrators. Women populate parish councils, lead sacramental formation, and take communion to the sick. Despite the great work women contribute to the Catholic Church, often as an unpaid or underpaid labor of love, they are relegated to second-class citizenship within the Church, as they are barred from ordination. Women have been told that they cannot represent Christ *in persona Christi* because they lack the anatomy of Jesus. Instead, women and girls are taught "complementarity," which is a way to claim that women have gifts all their own, different from men's gifts. Separate but most assuredly equal. Yet, this is not convincing to many women. Telling women that they cannot represent Christ to others through leadership and administering sacraments diminishes their personhood.[4]

That said, this is not a book about women's ordination. Nor does this book seek a head-on collision with the hierarchical structure of the Catholic Church. However, this book does intend to create space for women to name their experiences—whatever they might be—including space to claim their sense of call, even to ordination.

Historically, women have found spaces within the Church in which they exercised leadership and authority. Early Christian women opted for celibacy, which removed them from the patriarchal control of fathers and husbands. Women joined convents and eventually communities of women religious where they governed their own lives and responded to the needs of the day as they saw fit. Women turned to mysticism as a source of spiritual authority. Even still, women have had to be contortionists, trying to find a way to fit within the limited spaces allotted to them within the Church.

Catholic women have been strongly discouraged from voicing their experiences aloud and sometimes even silenced. John Paul II's apostolic letter *Ordinatio Sacerdotalis* attempts to end any possibility that women might be ordained by incorrectly insisting that women have never been ordained.[5] Women who speak out against clerical abuse have faced silencing tactics, from the excommunication of Mary MacKillop to attempts to preventing the publication of the reports of the sisters from India, Sisters Josephine Villoonnickal, Alphy Pallasseril, and Anupama Kelamangalathu, regarding sexual abuse in a #MeToo and #CatholicsToo world.[6]

However, women have all too often self-silenced themselves before others have the chance to shut them down. People stop short of naming the truth of their experience because they do not want to deal with the pushback they might receive. Sisters hold back from mentioning the state of women in the Church because they do not want to detract from the important ministries where they believe they can effect change. Women students hold back in discussions in theology classrooms because they know their thoughts will not be affirmed. Even the current movement calling for the women's deaconate may be an example of self-silencing. It seems like a case of women asking for what might be possible, with an indisputable history of women deacons supported by Scripture and history. The women's deaconate movement tiptoes around the ordination question and carefully clarifies that this is not about women becoming priests. This may be a strategy for moving things forward, but it does so by fitting women into too small of spaces. The silencing and self-silencing women experience continues. Yet, the Catholic Church's need to recognize women as fully human, called to follow and represent Jesus Christ, is not going away.

Despite everything, there are women who are fighting for a reason to stay. They are creative, energetic, gifted women who do create spaces for themselves within the Catholic Church. These pages provide space for women to name the complicated truth of their experiences. These women demonstrate that they can and do carve out spaces for themselves and others within the Catholic Church. They can ask hard questions, hold fast to their calls, and find ways to use their gifts. This book also suggests a path forward for continuing to create spaces for women in the Catholic Church.

THE EMERGENCE OF THIS BOOK

This book grows out of listening to the struggles of women in the parishes where I ministered in Iowa, Illinois, and Texas, as well as to young women studying theology in graduate school. Over and over, I hear laywomen name their struggles with serving, praying, leading, and remaining within the Catholic Church, and I realize that I share many of their challenges. The greatest difference between their experiences and mine seems to be that they often felt isolated and alone in their struggles, while I know that I have an entire network of sisterly support to rely upon to help me negotiate whatever difficulties I might face. When the bishop decided only men's feet would be washed on Holy Thursday, when the pastor treated Catholic school families very differently from religious education (that is, public school) families, when a new priest's leadership style involved fostering fear in the parish staff, I had an entire network of religious women I could call upon. Countless numbers of my sisters have negotiated tough situations in parishes and with clergy. They have been a source of wisdom and feedback. I have been aided by their willingness to strategize with me to find a way forward in many difficult clerical situations. My sisters help me name that clerical abuses of power are fundamentally contrary to the way of Christ in the Gospels. When the Church silences and sidelines women or ostracizes our LGBTQ siblings, it is not living up to the teachings of Jesus.

All of this practical ministerial support is enhanced by spiritual support. Women's religious life also creates prayer spaces that are not dominated by men, which has been another kind of nourishment for me over the years. Although women may have to wrestle with painful clerical situations, it is freeing to be able to pray in environments and using language honed by the creativity and inspiration of women.

In my experience, having a network of sisterly support is freeing. It helps me to create possibilities in impossible situations. Hearing the stories of my sisters who have struggled with similar issues within the Church strengthens me. Their stories remind me that I am not alone. Knowing that I am supported gives me the confidence to trust my ability to negotiate difficult church situations with integrity.

Listening to these laywomen led me to wonder: Is the situation for these struggling laywomen hopeless? Might there be some way I can share the wisdom and networks of support that have graced my life with these laywomen? Are women who are not called to religious life simply doomed to navigate their relationships with the Church and its clergy alone? Religious life is an incredible gift in my life; how am I sharing that gift with others—including laywomen? Am I not obligated to share the gifts I have been given with others?

As I pondered these questions, two things happened. First, I watched the documentary *RBG* about Ruth Bader Ginsburg. The documentary reflects on the tremendous contribution Ginsburg has made to the lives of women in the United States by simply taking the next logical, strategic step. By finding that next step and using her gifts wholeheartedly, Ginsburg transformed society for women in the United States. I remember sitting in the theater where the idea hit me like a ton of bricks: *How do we transform the situation for women in the Catholic Church? What's the next logical, strategic step?*

The second encounter that sparked this project of *Creating Spaces for Women in the Catholic Church* was that I learned of the possibility of receiving a grant available to women religious exercising leadership in some capacity. I asked if the project could also include laywomen. I drafted a proposal and received a grant from Giving Voice, a network of younger women religious. Giving Voice's primary mission is to create spaces for younger women religious to connect with one another, thereby strengthening and sustaining younger women religious as they continue to affirm their call. Yet, women religious have an invested interest in all women in the Church finding the sustenance they need.

SHAPING THIS PROJECT

Women I've encountered in graduate school make up a core group of the contributors to this project. I invited these women who have shared their struggles to join me in writing this book. From there we broadened the circle of conversation and included others. After receiving the grant, I invited potential contributors to participate in two retreats: a discernment retreat and a writing retreat. The discernment retreat introduced everyone to the concept of the project *Creating Spaces for Women in the Catholic Church*, and it offered an opportunity for people to brainstorm together around possible topics they might write about. We gathered again a few months later for a weeklong writing retreat, which provided days framed with prayer, substantial time for writing, and the opportunity for feedback and affirmation of each other's insights and gifts.

This collaborative approach to writing was modeled after the process used by Juliet Mousseau and me for *In Our Own Words: Religious Life in a Changing World*, in which thirteen younger women religious wrote about their experiences as younger women religious.[7] For *In Our Own Words*, we deliberately crafted a project in which we shaped each other's work. Instead of thirteen different, independent essays, we were also influenced by the reflections and experiences of the others. In *Creating Spaces*, the contributors similarly read and provided feedback on each other's work. Through our sharing, we formed a safe space where women could name their experiences *as women* within the Catholic Church. In some cases, this meant voicing their experiences aloud for the first time. The contributors may have had different experiences, yet they listened to one another without judgment. *Creating Spaces* is a more sensitive subject than *In Our Own Words*, as women have frequently felt there is no room for them to verbalize their hopes and struggles in the Church. During the discernment retreat, I believe every laywoman present came to me in tears as she thanked me for creating a space in which they were free to name their experiences and be heard. We created a sacred and liberating space for each other, which facilitated the sharing found within these pages.

WITHIN THESE PAGES

This book contains many examples of how women create spaces for themselves within the Catholic Church. The contributors highlight and engage their theological training as they reflect on their experiences. Their genuine searching and their courage shine through on every page as they ponder different facets of what it means to be women who carve out spaces for themselves within the Catholic Church.

In the opening chapter, Caroline Read shares her journey of discovering that she mediates the divine for herself as she searches for spiritual role models, finds God in the gift of tears, and engages in conversations with her mother. Read shares the sacred experience of realizing that she does not have to wait for someone to explain her own spiritual insights. In chapter 2, Silvana Arevalo reveals that the quest for God and happiness is ongoing. There is no point at which a person can say she has arrived. Instead, a deepening relationship with God unfolds over time—sometimes after heartrending searching and confusion. Next, Stephanie Boccuzzi offers her experience of "Learning to Speak the Language of Feminism in the Seminary Classroom," as she explores insights from women's experiences in the tennis world and the business world to make sense of the seminary classroom. Boccuzzi offers strategies for negotiating clerical spaces based on her experiences.

Then Mary Perez and Lisa Cathelyn in chapters 4 and 5 explore the effects of different organizations in offering safe spaces. Perez challenges the efficacy of the Fellowship of Catholic University Students (FOCUS) in providing meaningful spaces within campus ministry to BIPOC (Black, Indigenous, People of Color) students as she unpacks the limiting narratives FOCUS offers regarding what it means to be Catholic. Cathelyn then turns to The Dinner Party as an example of a secular organization that creates space for young people who have experienced loss—by breaking bread together. Cathelyn demonstrates that secular spaces can also be sacred. Then in chapter 6, Kristina Ortega exercises her baptismal call through her "Building the Domestic Church: Raising Children as a Progressive, Catholic, Mamá." Ortega provides a glimpse of a day in her life as she raises her children and cultivates an intentional faith-filled environment.

In chapter 7, Elaina Jo Polovick LeGault shares her journey of self-discovery through her call to create liturgical experiences, beginning as a teenager preparing a funeral liturgy for her grandmother. LeGault struggles with the limited role the Catholic Church offers for women and her own emerging sense of call to preside and lead. Through creating and leading meaningful prayer experiences, LeGault ultimately discerns there is no space for her to exercise her call within the Catholic Church.

Sarah Fariash, in chapter 8, draws on her experiences as a Catholic woman serving as a hospital chaplain as she considers larger questions within the Catholic Church. She understands the life and death she encounters in the hospital through the lens of paschal mystery—the life, death, and resurrection of Jesus. Fariash posits that the Catholic Church need not fear dying to that which is limiting to God's people, as resurrection has the last word.

Finally, in chapter 9, Sarah Kohles, OSF, addresses both laywomen and women religious as she suggests a way forward to offer greater support for women in the Catholic Church. She specifically encourages women religious to place their gifts at the service of laywomen and proposes that Giving Voice, a network of younger women religious, may serve as a model for networking among laywomen.

Creating space for laywomen to give voice to their experiences within the Catholic Church is essential for the health of the Church and for the effective handing on of the faith from one generation to the next. The women who share their stories within these pages point the way forward. They signal the need for change. They offer creative responses to their experiences of church. These women invite us to see our familiar church anew. Through their eyes, we consider new possibilities and opportunities for women within the Catholic Church.

NOTES

1. David Briggs, "U.S Women at Crossroads as Gender Gap Disappears: Will Pope Francis Make a Difference?" *The ARDA: Association*

of Religious Data Archives, September 25, 2013, http://blogs.thearda .com/trend/featured/u-s-catholic-women-at-crossroads-as-gender-gap -disappears-will-pope-francis-make-a-difference/.

2. Mark M. Gray and Mary L. Gautier, "Catholic Women in the United States: Beliefs, Practices, Experiences, and Attitudes," *The Center for Applied Research in the Apostolate*, 2018.

3. These comments were voiced to me during the Congregation of the Doctrine of the Faith's investigation of the Leadership Conference of Women Religious, viewed by many as an unfair critique of women religious in the United States. For a description of how the sisters responded to the investigation, see Annmarie Sanders, IHM, ed., *However Long the Night: Making Meaning in a Time of Crisis, A Spiritual Journey of the Leadership Conference of Women Religious* (Create Space Independent Publishing Platform, 2018).

4. Sr. Theresa Kane's 1979 address to Pope John Paul II on his first visit to the United States makes a similar point as she asserts that "the Church in its struggle to be faithful to its call for reverence and dignity for all persons must respond by providing the possibility of women as persons being included in all ministries in our Church." Theresa Kane, RSM, "Welcome to Pope John Paul II," 7 October 1979, Donna Quinn Collection 5/Pope's U.S. Visit - 1979, 1 of 3, Women and Leadership Archives, Loyola University, Chicago, IL, https://documents .alexanderstreet.com/d/1000690795.

5. Gary Macy, *The Hidden History of Women's Ordination: Female Clergy in the Medieval West* (Oxford University Press, 2007). Macy provides ample evidence that women have been ordained. Denying this reality is another form of silencing women and erasing their experiences from history.

6. Lila Rice Goldenberg, "#NunsToo: How the Catholic Church has Worked to Silence Women Challenging Abuse," *The Washington Post*, April 17, 2019, https://www.washingtonpost.com/outlook/2019/04/17/ nunstoo-how-catholic-church-has-worked-silence-women-challenging -abuse/.

7. Juliet Mousseau and Sarah Kohles, eds., *In Our Own Words: Religious Life in a Changing World* (Collegeville, MN: Liturgical Press, 2018).

Chapter 1

CLAIMING MY OWN SPIRITUAL AUTHORITY

Caroline Read

As a young woman in the Catholic Church, I easily shrink into my timidity and ask myself, *Who am I to claim the authority of leadership in this church?* When I look back on the small steps that I have taken in my professional and personal development, each one has brought me further into Catholic circles. My community, interests, and professional growth have been shaped and formed by each incremental movement forward. There are moments I look around in astonishment, thoroughly surprised by where my path has taken me. *How did I get here?* I wonder. And yet I know that this is where I am called, and here I stand: a millennial, Catholic woman, ambivalent about my religious identity at times, but unwilling to back down from claiming the legitimacy of my identity and voice in this community. With one foot in and one foot out, I am both in love with and thoroughly heartbroken by this faith tradition that continues to inspire and confound me. How can I stay? But how could I possibly go?

As a millennial Catholic who is grounded in a progressive faith and committed to social justice, I often find myself apologizing for my faith, taking one step toward the Church and two steps back, adding caveats when I claim my affiliation. I'm unsure how to embody my religious identity in my secular culture. Raised by baby boomer parents who remember the tumultuous changes in the Church in the wake of

Vatican II, I have learned to take the best my Catholic faith has to offer and disregard the teachings and practices that I do not agree with. By disengaging from instances of disagreement, I self-censor, leaving my opinions that don't agree with the Church outside of the sanctuary and beyond the tradition. In disengaging those parts of myself from my religious tradition, in this odd bifurcation of my Catholic identity, I let others' understanding of the Catholic faith define me. As I consider this strange dance, I wonder, *What if I were to stand where I am, in all of myself, without rejecting any parts of myself, and thoroughly claim my identity as a millennial, Catholic woman who sometimes disagrees with the Church?*

This question presents the possibility of exploring what this reclamation could look and feel like. I explored this question with the other authors of these essays, with whom I could openly name and delve into topics, opinions, and ideas that I usually set aside in Catholic spaces. With them, I felt a sense of empowerment and communion that encouraged me to more authentically name my experience. I felt fully seen in this community of women. I recognized myself in their stories and felt a sense of kinship in our shared experiences. In this space, without fear of retribution or misinterpretation, our identities, our hopes, and our desires could be fully expressed and brought into the light. It was in this space of sisterhood and brave possibility that I began to understand and recognize my own gifts. In the presence of these women, I experienced a small yet profound shift in my perspective and view of myself. It is with this clear understanding of self and sense of possibility that I forge ahead, clear-sighted and unafraid.

ENCOUNTERING A FOREMOTHER

As a woman raised in the Jesuit, Catholic tradition, I now find it odd that this order is not open to women religious. It did not used to matter to me—the possibility never occurred to me. It can be difficult to imagine another paradigm when you have yet to see an alternative. Growing up, my world was my Jesuit parish and elementary school, the same school attended by generations of my family and the same parish where countless family celebrations and sacraments have been held. Although I cannot say how exactly, perhaps just the alchemy of time spent in a place makes it become something more to you as you become a part of it too, but this parish of my childhood, community, family, and legacy is a distinct part of my identity.

When it came time to choose where I would attend college, I was drawn to attend a Jesuit university, feeling a sense of instant familiarity and kinship. At the Jesuit university in California that I attended, I experienced a love for academics, found a community, and felt supported in my burgeoning sense of possibilities for my life as my Jesuit education encouraged me to search for the "more."[1] It was this sense of possibility that led me to serve as a Jesuit volunteer in the Pacific Northwest, taking a giant leap into the Jesuit world, into community, into relationship and justice in a way that I could not know or fathom but already deeply desired. I felt a pull into this world. I admired the commitment, compassion, and centered calmness of those I met who had embraced Ignatian values, pedagogy, spirituality, and practice. In my admiration, I knew I deeply desired to be a part of it too.

During my two years as a Jesuit volunteer, and in the subsequent years spent serving people experiencing homelessness in Seattle, I felt called to further study, question, engage, critique, discover, rediscover, uncover, and fight with and for this religious tradition. I was intimidated and scared of the tenuous path I was setting upon. Despite these fears, I possessed a clarity that pursuing the academic resources and legitimacy to ask these questions this was something I needed to do. I longed to learn more about and find solace in the knowledge and leadership of fierce Catholic women. The examples of strong, faithful women in my family, Mary, and other biblical women, and Elizabeth Johnson's *She Who Is* had given me the conviction that there was so much yet to discover regarding women's legacy in the Church. I felt drawn to discover and preserve what I knew could be found beyond the thin veil of "history" to uncover a different sort of precedent.

During my first semester as a theology graduate student, I took the class "Women in the Reformation." We discussed women who had impacted and carried out the Protestant Reformation on their own terms. We studied their actions and words and addressed them seriously as theologians. While reading a secondary text for the class, "Women and Gender in Early Modern Europe," I stumbled across *one sentence* that addressed the existence of women Jesuits, naming Isabel Roser and Mary Ward. *Wait. Who?* I thought to myself. Never had I heard that term or those names. As a woman in her late twenties who had spent her whole life in Jesuit institutions, I was filled with energy and hope for what these women could mean to me. And so, for the class's final research paper, I took a deep dive into the life of Mary Ward, the woman who founded an order inspired by the Jesuits.[2]

Born in 1585 to a Catholic family in England, Mary's young years were shaped by the religious conflicts that dominated English society and politics in the wake of Henry VIII's break with the Roman Catholic Church. Her parents were in and out of prison for their confessional identity throughout her childhood, and her grandmother raised her at their family estate in the Yorkshire countryside.

During these years, Jesuit missionaries had begun to infiltrate England, supported and hidden away by recusant Catholic families such as Mary's. These families hid priests in their large, countryside estates to prevent their capture and execution. Therefore, Mary grew up in close proximity to religious life in general and Jesuits in particular. From an early age, she spoke of wanting to join a religious order. She did so at the age of twenty, going against her family's wishes, as they wanted her to stay in England and get married. However, she departed for St. Omer in the Netherlands, where persecuted English Catholics migrated and found refuge.

The Council of Trent, the Catholic Church's response to the Protestant Reformation, had instituted a number of restrictions on women's religious orders. They were to be enclosed, meaning that the members were cloistered and not to leave the convent, and convents fell under the authority of their local bishop. The Jesuits had a strong presence in St. Omer. Mary immediately sought them out upon arriving, and they directed her to join the Poor Clares. Mary struggled during these years in St. Omer. While outwardly successful, she recognized that being an enclosed nun was not where God was calling her. So, she left religious life and returned to England to continue to search for God's call in her life.

In London, Mary worked in the community, serving the poor, vulnerable, and imprisoned. Surrounded by a small group of women who were friends and relatives, she enacted her faith in serving those in need. It was during this time that Mary heard the voice of God tell her to "take the same as the Society." Her spiritual adviser was a Jesuit, and, when he heard of her experience, he provided her with the founding documents of the Society. Mary copied the document, changed a few pronouns, and set off to found her new Ignatian order.

Using the Jesuit's founding documents, Mary's new order was controversial in two important ways. First, like the Jesuits, these women ministered amongst society, meaning not in a cloistered convent. Second, also following the examples of the Jesuits, the new order would not report to the local bishop. Instead, their Superior General would report directly to the pope. Mary did not intend to be controversial. She saw a need in the community, felt God's call, listened intently, and responded. Even further, the model of religious life she sought already existed and was approved by the Vatican, as the Society of Jesus had become an officially recognized order about five decades prior.

Mary opened schools to educate girls and established communities as her unofficial order gained traction. Her community's work flourished, and she journeyed to Rome to receive approval from the Vatican. The approval process stretched out for years. At times it seemed that, despite these women's unpopularity (they were derisively referred to as "galloping girls" and their work was belittled from all sides), approval was within their grasp.[3] A commission of cardinals was formed to look into Mary's order and, when they reached a decision, Pope Urban VIII described this group of women as a "poisonous growth" that must be "suppressed, extinct, rooted out, destroyed, and abolished."[4] Mary was imprisoned for two months and spent the remaining years of her life under house arrest. Her order's communities and schools were closed. And yet...her companions kept her memory alive by writing her biographies, which served as continual inspiration in their work to strive to bring about Mary's vision. Communities and schools set up within Ward's network continued to thrive outside of the Vatican's reach. A small network of schools and communities continued for over a century without recognition from the Church, until the order received Vatican approval in 1703. The approval came with the explicit instructions that Mary Ward could not be cited as the order's foundress. Her memory and its ability to inspire still appeared to be too dangerous.[5]

Mary Ward was exactly what I had been searching for: a woman who had felt her call deeply and personally, who had been inspired by Ignatian spirituality, who created a new alternative space for women to do something different that had not previously been available to them. She had flown in the face of authority but had never seen herself as any more special or gifted than other women. This woman loved God. She loved God's people, and she keenly felt the pull to do something "more."

As I researched her, read her words, reflected on her in prayer, and shared her story with my classmates (and anyone else who would listen to me), the power of Mary Ward's story brought tears to my eyes. For not only is her life's work and her perspective on women's ministry remarkable, but her story demonstrated to me that women had come before me who had also struggled with their relationship to the Society of Jesus. Mary and her companions were formed by the spirituality, leadership, commitment to justice, and intellectual rigor of the Jesuits, though they had to navigate how to affiliate and relate to this fraternal organization.

With each step of my life, I have found myself moving progressively further into the institutional structures of the Church, which was not my anticipated direction. As a laywoman at a Jesuit theologate, surrounded by Jesuit priests and Jesuits in formation, I was both at home and so very far from home. Mary showed me how to trust and listen to this call, God's call, with patience, trust, and sincerity. For example, Mary circulated a letter to her sisters in response to the criticism of a bishop who declared that the community would soon meet its demise as they were "but women." She wrote,

> I would to God that all men understand this verity: that women, if they will, may be perfect, and if they would not make us believe we can do nothing, and that we are 'but women,' we might do great matters.[6]

While outspoken critics attempted to diminish her order's efforts, their words did not dampen Mary's vocation. During a time when women were seen as second-class citizens, Mary Ward insisted that women's abilities were equal to men's in the eyes of God. In this excerpt, Mary speaks to the damage of internalized misogyny and how community expectations and societal pressures can lead women to distrust and discount what they have to offer. It is with a sincere trust in God that women can reject these voices and listen to that small, still voice of God within themselves, bravely listening to where it leads them as they step out into the world to accomplish "great matters." I return to this quote frequently, always with a surprise and sadness at how applicable her words still are today. Despite the discouraging fact that these words are still so pertinent four hundred years later, I find a courageous permission therein. Women may do great matters, if only they trust themselves to do so.

WHAT WORDS OF SPIRITUAL TRUTH
DO I HAVE TO OFFER?

I recently coordinated a retreat and asked a Jesuit I know if he would facilitate. While he said yes, he turned the question back to me, asking me to help lead. With little choice in the matter, I agreed. My contribution consisted of the retreat talk, an articulation of how I experience God's love. The retreat was facilitated with Ignatian Yoga, an organization that seeks to blend yoga practices and Ignatian spirituality. The task of writing my talk nagged at me for weeks, a dull specter of anxiety looming in my future. I felt I had nothing to say and put off writing my talk. But I took the question, "How do I experience God's love?" seriously, mulling it over in quiet moments. I pondered my question, unable to articulate an answer quite yet. As the retreat date approached, I grew increasingly nervous. I questioned what I was doing and why I couldn't come up with something to say. I had to say something—there was no alternative.

What could I say that rings true to me? What could I say that is also honest and sincere and meaningful? What could I say about my experience that would not only be personally significant to me but would offer something to the people in attendance? I put it off and put it off and put it off. In the last forty-eight hours before the retreat, in the frantic last minutes of writing, I knew I had landed on something real. It flowed out of me on the Friday afternoon through the wee hours of Saturday morning before the day began. I typed out the finishing touches, printed it off, sat in front of the empty retreat room, and practiced reading it aloud. As I spoke the words to an empty room, measuring my speech and pace, my voice felt strong and my words sure. What I had written was what I wanted to say. It wasn't a clear answer, nor a didactic lesson, but a moment of lowercase *t* truth. I felt calm in this offering—my truth of small moments of experience, of glimmers of realizations still beyond my grasp, a woman yearning to struggle to realize God.

The time came, and I gave the talk without the panic I usually feel, the company of butterflies that sprout in my belly and gurgle in my throat when I speak to a crowd. I sat cross-legged on the floor and slowly spoke my piece, looking up and making eye contact with those who sat in the room with me. After I concluded and held a moment of silence, I quietly removed myself from the front of the room, eager for the focus to no longer be on me. A retreatant followed, an older woman around my mother's age. Wearing a cheerfully pink sweatshirt and kind eyes, she approached me, her expression sincere and her eyes brimming with tears. "Thank you," she whispered to me. "You're right, God's in all of us." We embraced and my throat constricted with emotion. Never once had I explicitly made that statement in my talk. I hadn't even articulated to myself that clearly what I had been circling around. But she had heard that message in my words, in my experience, in what I was trying to say. In sharing my one small lens in the kaleidoscopic view of God, she had heard this beautiful message. I was so grateful that she now shared it with me and allowed me to know what my efforts in attempting this spiritual leadership meant to her.

This is what I said:

> Tears come to me easily. Any experience of a strong emotion will often send my tear ducts into overdrive. Whether an emotional movie scene or a sentimental favorite song, I know when my soul resonates with something true—my tears tell me.
>
> More than in response to a movie or song, my tears usually come in response to moments of connection with others. It is in these moments when I am grateful for my tears. Whether in a moment of faith sharing with a small group, praying with roommates, or sharing in a moment of solace with a dear friend, the deep resonance of connection in these moments brings up a wellspring of emotion, which overflows out of me in tears.
>
> My tears clue me into my heart's response and connect me to the life around me. My tears are my guideposts to recognizing the divine in my life. Even as I write this sentence, I can feel my eyes start to swell and my throat constrict, recognizing the truth of what I've just admitted to myself.
>
> As I allow myself to sink into the memories of this past year, considering when I've had an experience of God, when I've felt a sense of God's unconditional love, mercy, and acceptance, I follow these tears. I know that these moments of emotion bursting forth, pricking my eyes, collapsing into my heart, and expanding outward, lead me to recall moments of encounter with the divine.
>
> This past June, I traveled to Kenya to see a dear friend and grad school classmate be ordained a Jesuit priest. A

whole group of us traveled to witness this important moment in his life. There were so many moments during that week in Nairobi that I could describe, when I felt this overflowing of emotion that points to my sense of connection to something beyond myself.

One moment that I will remember for the rest of my life was our night in the countryside. After a long day of travel, the seven of us gathered together before dinner to celebrate Mass. Ordained a priest only a few days before, Oscar celebrated his first Mass for our group in the grassy knoll next to our cabins. Under the twilight sky, as a crescent moon slowly rose, the six of us perched on a cement half-wall facing our friend as he celebrated with us his first Mass. As he confidently and humbly shared this gift with our small group, coming into this moment that he had so long prepared for, I felt the Spirit's presence in our celebration, and the meaning for my friend as he more fully came into his vocational call. The beauty of the moment grasped my heart and tears sprung to my eyes as I witnessed Oscar offer to the world that to which God was calling him.

But what about me? I find it easier to recognize these moments of transcendence as the Spirit moves in the lives of others. It is much more difficult to recognize and name these movements in my own life. But I follow the memories of my tears, and they lead me to name and perceive God's love and presence already functioning within me.

About a month ago, I had the opportunity to go on retreat with about a dozen other young Catholic women like myself. We gathered at the Jesuit Retreat Center in Los Altos, nestled in the hills above Silicon Valley. In the afternoon, we paired up, walking and talking as we delved further into the graces of the morning.

A woman named Mary had been standing next to me, so when prompted to find a partner, we turned to each other and headed out on our walk, tracing slow, meandering circles across the property of the Los Altos retreat center.

As we began our meditative movement, slowly tracing the curvature of the rounding green hill behind our retreat house, Mary, in the most straightforward manner, posed a question to me: "Can you tell me more about what you meant when you spoke this morning? I'm interested."

While I had shared with our large group my feelings of inadequacy around my Catholic faith and practice, it was in Mary's unassuming, welcoming, and unconditionally non-judgmental presence that I felt at ease to share a little more. She probed, asking the questions I am often too afraid to confront in a real way.

When I finished sharing, I felt the sourness of shame in my stomach and anxiety twist in my lungs. But Mary responded with an understanding smile as she looked at me, and it was okay. The burn of embarrassment and shame in admitting these things aloud, met with nothing but uncon-ditional acceptance. It transformed the slow burn of the fear that I don't believe well enough, that my faith isn't enough, and that my connection to God must be weaker than oth-ers'. It was okay. I was okay. I was enough. Without blinking, Mary entered with me into my self-doubt and shame.

In this moment, as she stood next to me, I realized that I feared that as soon as I revealed these things to her, her opinion of me would change. But it didn't. And her unconditional regard, her loving acceptance, brought fast tears to my eyes. Her steady, loving presence manifested a greater sense of this presence to me. In that moment, I felt this unconditional, loving presence, understanding in a new way God's love for me. Perfect belief, perfect practice is not required to experience God's love. As I felt the depth of this fleeting moment twist my heart open, rotating my percep-tion of the world and of the divine presence available to me into something new, my eyes brimmed with tears.

RECOGNIZING SOMETHING NEW

"You don't want to be a priest," my mom declared, or perhaps clarified, as we began our phone call. I don't remember what topic we were discussing that had prompted her to say this. But it was nothing out of the ordinary. Our conversations often turn to church and church politics.

"Well…," I felt the need to interject, the first time I've ever done so.

When I was a junior in high school, I was confirmed. My mother stood in for my sponsor, a welcome, calming presence as I sat in the very front pew. After confirming us all, the bishop paced the width of the altar in front of the pews. "Who among you will answer the call?!" he bellowed. "Who among you will answer the call to become a priest?!"

My mother softly nudged my side and whispered to me, "Raise your hand."

Now, I don't think she was serious; she was just making a point about protest, struggle, and equality to her daughter. But I don't know. I've never asked her about it. Perhaps, at the age of seventeen, she saw something in me that I did not yet see in myself.

So here I was on the phone with her, trudging up a steep grade as I made my way up the Berkeley hills, the soft, grey clouds slowly settling into the San Francisco Bay as the day's light dimmed. Over a decade later I respond, "I don't know, Mom."

I've been asked this question in the years between, by her, by friends, by a spiritual director, by a Jesuit priest. I always turned the question down, explaining that "while women's ordained ministry is important to me as a justice issue, I myself do not feel 'the call.'" My mother was taken aback at my answer, markedly different from what I usually say. I refused to let my answer be definitive—an unprecedented response from her daughter. I felt that saying "no," or even implying it, would be an insult to the slow crack of light I was beginning to let in: the possibility that God has called me and entrusted me with gifts to share.

Even though our conversation had been on a different path, we veered, and I hurriedly attempted to explain what—to me—felt almost unexplainable. Not much had changed, really; but in this new season of my adult life, I was understanding moments of deep meaning, connection, and transcendence as God being with me.

As I told my mother, nothing had changed, really—I was just examining it from a different vantage and seeing it for what it is for the first time. For so many years, I've felt myself pulled into this religious world, almost by accident, but it has always resonated and confirmed something within me, so I continued taking steps into this world. I always felt a hesitancy, a sense of imposter syndrome, not feeling like I should or deserved to be there. But these moments led me to recognize the undeniable pull—call—that I have been answering and confirming. God's love and grace are leading me, available to me, and radiating from me. In this journey that I am taking, who am I to negate a possibility?

This pause of consideration was the first time I voiced this difference to my mother. I grasped for an explanation as I blindly attempted to articulate what this difference even was, even if it functionally made no difference at all. Finally, I landed on the perfect metaphor.

"It's like a geoduck!" I exclaimed, proud to have landed on such a perfect analogy.

I had recently landed on describing my spirituality, my relationship with God, as skittish, like a cat. But suddenly, this metaphor came to me, and it was so much better.

I grew up in the Pacific Northwest, and during the summers, my family would often spend time on Whidbey Island, where my grandparents had built a small cabin on the southwest shore. On perfect August days, with the white-capped, dusty purple Olympic Mountains rising beyond the still saltwater of the sound, our beach would be revealed by the slow, measured progress of the tide.

Tide pools teemed with hermit crabs in barnacle-y shells, dark messes of seaweed, prized sand dollars, and small fish. Walking along the tide flats, along these shallow pools and dodging rough stone, one comes across small, raised holes in the sand. Like a kid stepping on every line of the sidewalk, growing up we would aim to let our pounding footsteps land squarely on these small holes, eager for the event our footsteps' pressure might cause. For buried in the sand under these holes are geoducks, a very large sort of mollusk with an unfortunate appearance. With the right land of a footstep, the geoduck squirts water as its one line of attack. As kids we would delight in this momentary engagement, a clue that something was there beneath the surface, beyond our line of sight, but reacting to and playing with us. With the miniature squirt of water cluing us in to what could be found below, we would dig in the sand.

Digging for geoducks is difficult, and I have never successfully caught one. As you dig, water fills the hole as the geoduck sinks further into the sand, evading the effort to find it.

This is my relationship to God. *This* is how I can understand these fleeting moments that I know, moments that catch my attention, clue me in that there's something there, something special happening; it's not just another step on the sand. So, I stop and start to dig. But the more I try, the more I dig, the more I search, the more the hole fills with murky water, getting in my way and making my progress less clear and much more effortful. This thing doesn't want to be found, to be seen.

About a month after this phone call with my mother, I told this story and metaphor to a mentor and friend. "My relationship with God is like a geoduck!" She intently listened and laughed and celebrated with me my discovery of a moment of language to describe my relationship to the divine. Then she paused. "What if," she said, "God's not the geoduck? What if, instead, you are the geoduck and God is searching for you?"

In this moment of her saying so, I remembered an imaginative prayer experience that has stayed with me over the years. *Picture yourself in a place you love.* I imagined myself sitting on a log on that beach on Whidbey Island, staring across the water to the peninsula where those sharp mountain peaks rise, the gentle lap of the tidal waves shh-hhhsshing along the shore and in my ear. *Now,* the exercise prompted, *see yourself as God sees you.* And in my mind's eye, from quite a distance above, I saw myself standing on that beach, shoulders slightly hunched, carefully holding my arms across my body, tentatively standing where I was.

"Oh, honey," I breathed in my mind, a sympathy and gratitude and prayer for self-assurance and courage coursing through me. "You're okay," I whispered.

WHERE IS THIS MOMENT LEADING ME?

I feel this possibility brewing inside of me. *What happens when I begin to peel back the layers of authority, institution, doctrine, and language? What will still be there within this institution that inspires and demonstrates the divine? What glimmer of recognition of the divine exists beyond the rules and restrictions, pomp and circumstance, which define this faith tradition? What is this spark, that deep gut feeling that pulls me onward and beyond?* When I start with that feeling, I can recognize the truth of which we are speaking. With heart-centered, sensate, emotive experience, I am beginning to connect to what I've heard people speak of my whole adult life. It's a "coaxing it out of me" type of process. This transcendent divine is skittish, like a cat. It doesn't want to be courted or understood or broken down into logical, verbalized words. It's beyond the words I learned growing up, the memorized prayers required for sacrament, beyond a rudimentary explanation of another person's theology. When I set these things aside and let myself begin with the experiences that are more to me, I begin to think that maybe, just maybe, I too believe in God.

In my first spiritual direction session, my spiritual director asked to pray aloud with me...and I just couldn't. *How could I verbalize my internal life when my understanding of God and religion had always been intellectually articulated to me? How could I begin to relate the mundane particularities of my life to a God whose care and connection I questioned?* I balked. But when I experience moments of real connection, I feel the growing sense of something beyond myself. It's when I let go and set aside what I've been told to intellectually understand, that I've begun to develop this sense, this sensitivity.

So, what has stopped me from doing this for so long? Fear. I'm afraid to speak out. I feel like I must have the "right" answer to legitimately say anything. It feels absurd to admit, but I'm *worried* about dogma and heresy and excommunication. I now recognize the fear in how I've always approached this religion that I love.

What if I step aside from all those dynamics of approval? What if I recognize that I mediate the divine—for myself, for my community, and in the world? I don't need approval or hierarchical avenues to access moments of transcendence. I can and do bring God into the world.

Any sort of statement like this makes me nervous. I immediately question: Does that go against the Church's teaching? Will I get in trouble? *Jesus Christ, I get in my own damn way.*

What if I reflect on these things without this worry? What real transformative possibility could open to me if only I allowed myself to sink into and marinate in the possibility of this personal, immediate, consecrated, real, tangible life of moments of the Divine revealed to me and *through* me?

NOTES

1. Magis, or "more" as it's translated from Latin is a common Jesuit term. Barton Geger, SJ, defines *magis* as "the more universal good." Barton Geger, SJ, "What Magis Really Means and Why It Matters," Jesuit Higher Education 1, no. 2 (2012): 16:31, https://www.xavier.edu/jesuit resource/resources-by-theme/documents/WhatMagisReallyMeans PublishedCopy.pdf.

2. I learned a great deal about Mary Ward and her life from many resources, especially M. Immolata Wetter, CJ, *Mary Ward under the*

Shadow of the Inquisition (Oxford, England: Way Books, 2006); Christina Kenworthy-Browne, CJ, ed., *Mary Ward (1585–1645) 'A Brief Relation,' with Autobiographical Fragments and a Selection of Letters* (Rochester, NY: The Boydell Press, 2008); and Christine Burke, IBVM, *Freedom, Justice and Sincerity: Reflections on the Life and Spirituality of Mary Ward* (Hindmarsh, South Australia: ATF Press, 2009).

3. Wetter, *Mary Ward under the Shadow of the Inquisition*, 21.

4. Pamela Ellis, "'They Are But Women': Mary Ward, 1585–1645," in *Women, Gender and Radical Religion in Early Modern Europe*, ed. Sylvia Brown (Leiden, The Netherlands: Koninklijke Brill, NV, 2007), 243.

5. The Institute of the Blessed Virgin Mary, the legacy of Ward's order, is the name of the congregation as approved by the Vatican in 1703. During Ward's life, her community of sisters was known as "the Institute" or referred to as the English Ladies.

6. Burke, *Freedom, Justice and Sincerity*, 9.

Chapter 2

BECOMING FULLY HUMAN

My Search for God and Happiness

Silvana Arevalo

El corazón no descansa en los placeres del mundo, en los honores, en las cosas, sino en Dios, en su Amor.

> Padre Jaime Bonet, *fundador de la
> Fraternidad Misionera Verbum Dei*

The heart does not rest in the pleasures of the world, in honors, in things, but in God, in God's Love.

> Father Jaime Bonet, founder of the
> Verbum Dei Missionary Fraternity

I began to seek to grow in faith a few years after graduating college when I was twenty-four years old. While I was raised Catholic, attended Catholic school from kindergarten through eighth grade, and received all the sacraments through confirmation, I knew very little about Catholicism. "Being Catholic" meant going to Mass, occasionally reciting prayers, and following the "rules": *Don't lie. Don't have sex before marriage. Do the right thing.* I didn't know much about Jesus, the Bible, or spirituality. A Maryland transplant in San Francisco working as an engineer, I also didn't have any friends who were Catholic. Most importantly, I had never experienced an encounter with God. (Or at least I had not learned how to recognize such an encounter.) I was what I would now label as "culturally Catholic." Challenged over the years by the skepticism of my peers, my faith was minimal; I doubted whether God really existed. Yet, the desire to believe in God and to experience God's presence remained within me, a seed planted from when I was young. As a child, my mom would often exclaim, "Thank you, Lord; thank you, Lord! God is so good to me!" for any little blessing in her day. An immigrant from Ecuador, my mom believed that she had overcome poverty and hunger because God was an active protector and provider. I admired her faith and thought it was beautiful.

Growing up, I loved going to Mass at my Catholic K–8 school. Uplifting songs like "Lord of the Dance" and "Bring Forth the Kingdom" were a joy to sing along to; I would leave Mass happy. However, when it came time to choose a high school, I chose the option with the best academic reputation, which happened to not be Catholic. At my new school, my peers criticized Catholicism as narrow-minded and intolerant, especially toward LGBTQ people. While challenged to grow in my thinking, I felt that I needed to hide my unpopular affiliation to avoid the stigma. Attending Mass in Spanish at the local parish with my family and no longer enjoying school liturgies now meant that I did not worship in my preferred language, nor at a Mass that was tailored to my age group. Also, staying up late doing my homework meant that I no longer prayed at night with my mom. I wasn't aware of it at the time, but all these factors contributed to the languishing of my Catholic identity and faith.

In college, I wanted to believe in God and practice my faith, so despite not having friends who were Catholic, I continued to go to Mass. However, I began to doubt whether God existed, as I lacked a sense of my own experience of God to ground my belief.

I also broke one of the "bigger" rules, leading to a break with what I considered a core element of being Catholic. For me, God was a God who was primarily interested in whether I followed the rules. The rule of "waiting until marriage" seemed like it was one of the most important rules to God, based on the sense of shame my family warned would be heaped upon women who broke that rule. Waiting until marriage was talked about more than any other moral issue. While I tended to do as I was told, this was one case in which my desires were stronger than I wanted to resist. In the moments I couldn't avoid the tension, I wondered: *What did God think? Could I still consider myself Catholic?*

I didn't know what to do about the disparity between what I understood as God's expectations and my failure to uphold this rule. With whom could I talk about my struggles? My questions about God, desire, and sex reemerged again and again in my adult years as I longed for companionship and connection. I deeply longed for love, and, at that point in my life, I found nothing in the Mass or in any religious activity that fulfilled my longing. If I were honest with myself, my romantic relationships weren't fulfilling me either, but I hoped that someday one would. How does God see me and my situation? What was so wrong about sex anyway? Are these not common and critical questions that many people are asking, especially when it comes to sex and sexuality?

My experience over the years seemed to confirm that, when it comes to sex, there are few safe spaces in which to authentically struggle and to discern God's presence and response in the struggle. Catholic spaces seemed to only offer silence, avoidance, or condemnation. Therefore, God only seemed to offer silence or condemnation. Absent from these spaces were dialogue and accompaniment rooted in compassion and understanding. It would take more than ten years after I first began to ask these questions to discover what the words *compassionate* and *merciful* meant, and that these were characteristics of God. Back then, I could not fathom any response from God other than indifference or condemnation.

Fifteen years later, and as recently as 2019, a priest compared me to an opened and soiled gift during confession. Thankfully, by then, I knew that nothing I did, nor anything a person of religious authority said, could change the crucial and central truth of our faith: I possess an inherent dignity as a human person who is loved by God. Because of the journey I had made in my spiritual life, I was more deeply rooted in my true and deepest identity as beloved and in God's unconditional love and presence. The shock and pain I felt from the priest's words did not lead to spiraling shame and despair. Though I was stunned that such disparaging language was still being used in 2019, I was also afraid of how many young people would be subjected to such language, especially since the church was close to a university. Would young people know that no matter what they did, God always loves them? Would they be able to turn to God and see eyes filled with love and compassion rather than disgust and judgment? Would it take a long time for other young people to understand that God is more merciful and understanding than the condemnation and judgment offered by many church leaders?

Instead of the church, my therapist provided the safest space to talk about sex. She accompanied me in embracing sexual desire as a part of my humanity, which was also affirmed by poetry I read by mystics and the Song of Songs. A rare and open conversation with an older, consecrated laywoman also showed me this, as she shared with me her own experience of praying with her puzzling feelings of attraction to another. While she found her feelings surprising and confusing, God did not. Instead, God reminded her, "You are still a woman," which calmed her apprehension. Accepting my sexual desires as part of my humanity was only the first step. It took me a few more years to discover that at the core of my desire for sex, more than pleasure, more than having fun, more than feeling attractive, was my deep longing to be loved by another. This longing could not be fulfilled by another person, no matter how much I wished. My longing was such that only the graced moments of intimacy with God in prayer could fulfill it. If the Samaritan woman in John 4 really did have multiple lovers, Jesus' response to her was not to condemn her but to offer his very self to her. He longed to offer her the path to discover her own spring of water within "welling up to eternal life" (John 4:14). It would take years to discover God, who fulfills and sustains, within me and to encounter God intimately in prayer.

After graduating from university, Mass at my local parish lacked meaningful preaching, and I stopped going. In my early twenties, I felt the most disconnected from my Catholic faith.

While I did feel a sense of estrangement and a loss of part of my identity, I had other priorities and pleasures that consumed my focus and attention. Given my parents' culture and history, my primary concerns growing up were my family and ensuring my survival through education and a career. My parents had sacrificed much to provide my brothers and me with the education and opportunities we had, opportunities that could only be dreamed of in their home country of Ecuador. Their sacrifices and hard work, as well as my dedication, paid off. I graduated from M.I.T. and gained a professional job at my dream company in an amazing city. I thought I had it all: financial security, an exciting position at a company I admired for their mission, validation and status in society, friends, and access to all the delights that popular culture seemed to equate with happiness—nice clothes, restaurants, trips, shows, clubs. Despite my achievements and the momentary highs that I experienced from my successes, social life, and romantic relationships, I often felt unfulfilled and sad. One evening after work, I rode the Caltrain to meet my boyfriend, at the time, for dinner. Sitting in the upper level, looking out on the trees and streetlights that passed by, an unexpected sadness within me brought me to tears. I called my mom, and when she asked me what was wrong, I told her the truth. I didn't know. Nothing unusual had happened. I was working long hours, but I was no stranger to stress and hard work. Why did I feel this way?

A few months later, my boyfriend and I broke up, and the pain of loss and anxiety about my life and my future overwhelmed me. To my dismay, I had found my new job at my dream company unfulfilling, but I couldn't imagine any other career that would be a good fit for me. I missed my family and friends back home, but it was hard for my twenty-four-year-old self to imagine leaving San Francisco's weather and creative culture. I was terrified of not finding the person I wanted to spend the rest of my life with. My anxiety intensified with my certainty that none of these problems were going to be resolved anytime soon.

In an effort to regain control of my life, I resolved to make some new priorities. The thought of going back to church had been nagging me for a few years. While I didn't really know what that meant other than going back to Mass on Sundays, deciding to act upon that nagging thought felt like the right thing to do. I resolved to take a break from dating. Instead, I dedicated my time and focus to finding my happiness in parts of myself I had let fall away. No longer believing in the American Dream, nor trusting popular culture, nor even my own desires that had ended in disillusionment, I anxiously searched for truth. What does it mean to live a good life? How does a person find happiness?

SEARCHING FOR HAPPINESS IN THE CHURCH

As with any commitment, I dove into my search with intensity. A Google search led me to a Dominican parish with more meaningful preaching and numerous faith formation programs. Through the parish, I discovered a program called "Landings" for Catholics returning to the Church. However, when I finished the program feeling the same as when I had started it, I was unsure of what I had gained. I longed to hear personal testimonies, concrete ways that God was present in people's lives, as I lacked my own sense that God existed. While the homilies and talks at my church were informative and interesting, I needed to hear speakers share in a way that made God real, present, personal, and intimate. The rare few who spoke affectively about God captivated me as they shared the ways in which they encountered God. I so deeply appreciated such heartfelt talks that I wanted to give such talks myself. However, I dismissed my aspiration as unrealistic and unattainable; I didn't know enough about the faith to be able to preach.

I also sought community as I embarked on my faith journey, hoping to share the journey with others. There were few options among those closest to me, as my family lived across the country, none of my work friends were Catholic, and few of my Catholic peers shared my curiosity about the faith. Instead, I reached out to Protestant Christian friends, who became my companions and guides as I searched for God. In that time, I considered joining a friend's small, young, and vibrant Protestant church. Visiting his church, I was surprised and touched by the community's friendliness and warm welcome. Though I was new, I felt seen, and my presence valued as opposed to the seemingly indifferent crowd at Mass. I was profoundly moved when their members immediately invited me to one of the neighborhood community groups that met weekly for Bible study and faith sharing. In their church, I witnessed what I longed for, the dedication and commitment to growing in faith both individually and as a community. As I met more members, I discovered that several were former Catholics. While the reasons for their conversions were not shared, I ultimately knew where I stood. As much as I deeply appreciated my friend's church and longed for a similar experience in the Catholic Church, converting to another religion was too great of a change for me to make at the time.

Despite often being the youngest by decades, and at times the less-than-welcoming culture, I kept participating in my church's programs and resolved to grow in the Catholic faith. One year later, I was invited to join a faith-sharing group with other Catholics who were closer to my age. For the first time, I experienced God's grace being poured out in community, as one person's insights and experiences resonated with another's and that person's with another's, and so on. It was a joy to connect with peers through their questions and struggles with faith.

For two years, I did everything I could think of to grow in my faith, hoping to find a solution within Catholicism to my persisting sadness. After sharing my ongoing struggle with a friend, she recommended I try going on a retreat. I didn't know what a retreat was, but I took her advice and found one starting the very next evening.

FINDING JOY

That weekend, I experienced what I so deeply longed for and had been searching for. Pleading for God to take away my sadness, I knelt before the Eucharist in the empty chapel at the Jesuit Retreat Center. I opened my Bible to Luke's account of the Annunciation, and I attempted to pray through *lectio divina* for the first time. As I read the passage, Mary's fear resonated with my own. In that moment of connection with the Word, my ongoing and persistent sadness dissipated. I was filled with the most beautiful feeling, which I knew I could never create on my own. While I cannot completely describe what I felt, it was like an inner sweetness, a wonderful joy. The experience convinced me that God existed at a depth within me that no rational argument had reached. It was my first experience of intimacy with God.

Alive with my discovery of the liberating power of a personal encounter with God, I felt impelled to share the experience. I wanted others to discover what I had discovered. However, I lacked the courage to share with my peers, as I had never heard anyone share such an affective spiritual experience. Outside of a faith-sharing group, conversations about God and sharing experiences of God in prayer were rare.

My experience convinced me of the power of praying with Scripture, the presence of God in the Eucharist, and silent retreats. Discovering that *lectio divina* helped me overcome my ongoing sadness persuaded me that the Catholic faith offered spiritual tools that would lead to my happiness. Then, I suddenly found myself organizing *lectio divina* prayer groups at my parish after expressing an interest in them. As I hoped, friendships deepened through sharing meals and sharing faith. The women in my *lectio* group challenged me and taught me valuable lessons. One evening a participant listened as I struggled to understand how I could receive the life that Jesus promises, and exasperated, she responded, "You find your life by losing it!" Her words resonated within me as I recognized Jesus' teaching from the Gospels. While humbling, I appreciated her willingness to point out a gospel value that I had yet to internalize, reaffirming the importance of community for the building up of faith.

MEETING VERBUM DEI

Within the same year following my retreat experience, three different friends encouraged me to check out Verbum Dei, a community of missionary sisters who hold Scripture-based prayer groups and retreats in the Mission District in San Francisco. Verbum Dei offered exactly what I was hoping for in a prayer group experience: song, preaching, and silent prayer with Scripture in community and in the presence of the Eucharist.

To give some background, *La Fraternidad Misionera Verbum Dei*, or Verbum Dei Missionary Fraternity, is a Catholic contemplative-active community, founded by diocesan priest Fr. Jaime Bonet in 1963 in Mallorca, Spain.[1] The Verbum Dei community writes of their ministries:

> We are committed to bringing the Gospel to life by inviting people into an intimate relationship with a loving God. Through contemplative prayer with Scripture and meditation by the way of weekend workshops, weekly sessions, or longer retreats, Verbum Dei encourages participants to engage in a life-giving, transformative journey of faith.[2]

The mission of the Verbum Dei is "prayer and ministry of the Word" (Acts 6:4), often through prayer groups and retreats. While I valued my *lectio divina* prayer group, I was still searching for what I had experienced on my retreat.

While in theory, Verbum Dei's ministries sounded exactly like what I was seeking, in reality, my initial experiences with the community were frustrating as a fledgling Catholic. Even though I had experienced a powerful moment of grace through *lectio divina*, I had little experience practicing it. I didn't know what spirituality or contemplation were. My analytical, problem-solving mindset had no patience for metaphors nor trust in imagination. My first retreat with Verbum Dei, titled "The Well Within," left me feeling bewildered and thinking, *I have no idea what just happened.* Unlike the retreats I had made with Jesuits where I walked away feeling like I had learned something moving or experienced something powerful, I didn't understand most of what the sisters had preached. I also felt nothing. Hearing other retreatants share their experiences of Jesus meeting them in their prayer when I hadn't experienced anything stirred up deep insecurities as I compared my experience to theirs. To me, God's silence meant absence, a very painful thought that could lead to despair. What was I doing wrong? What was I missing? My greatest strengths involved getting things done, so it was a new and very difficult experience to find myself unable to "achieve" prayer. Perceiving myself to be the only one struggling, I felt unable to share my struggles, which further exacerbated my sense of being alone on my journey.

Believing that my struggles could be overcome if I kept trying, I continued to participate in Verbum Dei's offerings. Over the next four years, I deepened my relationship with the Verbum Dei charism as I lived in community as part of their discernment program[3] and then in the novitiate. Verbum Dei became the community in which I first began learning to pray. The huge endeavor of developing my prayer life included struggling with difficult emotions like sadness or anger by reading the Psalms or singing laments, trying not to go crazy in the silence by letting go of anxious thoughts, and resting in God's loving presence in the present moment. Such practices were unfamiliar and challenging, but eventually I found them consoling. Not really knowing what it meant to pray, I wondered, *Is this what is supposed to happen?* Imaginative prayer continued to be beyond my analytical mind's ability to grasp. Jesus did not speak to me face-to-face as He spoke to other sisters; yet I discovered that God spoke to me through perceptions, intuitions, and my sense of the Holy Spirit within me. A line from Scripture or something a sister shared in a preaching would resonate within me, and I knew God wanted to say something. In the novitiate, I loved consistently being woken up by the Spirit before our alarm and the hectic rush to morning prayer—my stolen time alone with God in the calm and quiet of the early morning as I lay in bed. I loved reflecting upon Scripture passages, preparing a message to preach, and asking questions as Something within me responded with answers. These precious moments of grace contrasted with my daily "prayer" in the chapel where I analyzed, problem solved, or strove for an experience of God. God caught me by surprise when I was empty of my own agenda, having woken up from the surrender of sleep and simply resting in God.

While it took some years for the seeds that were being planted within me to grow and take root, Verbum Dei changed the ways that I imagined God. One of the sisters shared with me her faith and experience of a gentle and very close God, which contrasted with the impatiently demanding, distant, and indifferent God that I feared at times. She introduced me to the notion of prayer as talking with God about what was on her mind and in her heart, and she encouraged me to do the same. Her words stayed with me as I began to open up to the truth they contained. Desiring closeness to God, I deeply appreciated living in a home with a chapel containing the Eucharist. Having a sacred space dedicated to silence and stillness invited me to share my life more intimately with God. In the community, I entered into a rhythm of life centered on daily prayer and weekly morning retreats.

During the discernment program, I also participated in Verbum Dei's ministries, including a confirmation retreat given to mostly Latina teenagers in Long Beach, California. Coming from families with limited resources, many girls had not gone to Catholic schools, and this was their first retreat experience, made possible through sponsorship by the parish. The retreat was held at a campsite in the mountains, the first time many of the teenagers had traveled outside of the city. That weekend I noticed the transformation that took place within the students. Many of them did not want to be there, and yet they departed filled with joy. Even more, I was surprised by the transformation within me. While the retreat aimed to articulate the truths of faith in a way that the teenagers could understand and connect with, the retreat experience also met me so perfectly where I was in my own journey. The talks focused on the foundational truths of Christian faith, including that God is Love, God offers us unconditional love, and that our life's purpose is to love. These talks were reinforced by the students' receiving a letter from God compiled from passages like Isaiah 43:4, "You are precious in my eyes, and honored, and I love you." The students also wrote and burned their confessions, an act of trust in God's endless mercy. The retreat included a video and talk about body image, including a discussion of the role of the media and sexism, a topic that I felt was both relevant and important, and had never heard addressed in a religious setting. Finally, the teenagers who had returned as volunteers gave witness to the much-needed community they had found with each other. Retreatants expressed the desire to return and serve future retreatants because of the intimate friendship and support they saw during the retreat.

Toward the end of the first day of talks, games, and activities, the lights went out and music began to play as the retreatants cried out in recognition of a popular song. By the time the Mexican line dance, "Caballo Dorado," played, retreatants and leaders were on the dance floor together. Brimming with joy as I followed the steps, I thought to myself, *This is the best retreat ever!* Inspiring teens to discover a loving God, soaking in the peaceful stillness of the surrounding trees and mountains, laughing, and expressing Latinx culture spoke to the different parts of me that sought to be integrated in my budding new life with God. Any sadness or anxiety I had carried into the retreat dissipated as this retreat space gave me permission to be my whole self.

In that Verbum Dei retreat, I found what I had been searching for, an encounter with God and a mission that I could deeply believe in, helping others to encounter God, too. For my next mission, I was asked to preach to adults in Spanish, the language I had only used with family. It didn't matter whether I felt capable or ready, the Verbum Dei sisters insisted. Both excited and nervous, I gave it my all. I wanted everyone to find what they were searching for in God, as I had in those rare grace-filled moments of prayer. Through prayer groups and retreats, I wanted to provide others with the space and environment to encounter and experience God and God's love.

ENTERING VERBUM DEI

However, in the years leading up to my time in Verbum Dei, I had been longing for friendship with other Catholics, and my struggles continued in the community. Larger community gatherings and celebrations were often a joy, dispelling the negativity within me as lighthearted stories and laughter were shared. But learning to live a vowed life in community was complicated and presented many challenges. Poverty meant I could no longer buy take-out instead of cooking. Obedience meant my time was no longer my own. Furthermore, I struggled to form the friendships I had hoped for among the sisters. The lack of connection and sense of rejection from my peers activated my deepest insecurity: *There is something wrong with me.*

However, there were signs before Verbum Dei that the pressure I was placing upon myself was having a negative impact, most obviously on my physical health. I came down with shingles and unexplainable chest pains. I decided to take it down a notch at work, but my inner critic and taskmaster continued to push me in other areas like trying to lose weight and growing in my faith as a Catholic. The perfectionistic demands I placed on myself grew as I projected these attributes upon God. My "prayer time" often revolved around trying to perceive what God wanted me to do. My faith was centered on my successes or failures to meet these expectations rather than growing in friendship with God, because I thought that's what God cared about. The demanding, critical voice within me was the one I listened to and trusted most. It was difficult to hear any other. Having motivated myself through being hard on myself, the concept of gentleness as a virtue was foreign to me. I remember visiting the Verbum Dei sisters in Quito, Ecuador, with my family when I was in the novitiate. One of the sisters shared with me that one of the values they emphasize in their cultural context is *ternura* or tenderness. Her words rang true within me; *ternura* sounded like what I needed to develop within me. I also needed to open myself to seeing tenderness as an attribute of God.

However, the reality of being part of the community was that the missionaries were very active and there was always work to do. I supported the missionary efforts in various ways from cooking and cleaning for back-to-back retreats to putting down stone pavers at the new retreat center under construction. This type of work was unfamiliar to me, and I did not enjoy it. Ashamed of my emotions, I feared being judged as lazy.

I struggled to find joy in the manual labor. My ingrained inner expectations of doing my work quickly and well drowned out the potential quiet delight I might have experienced in chopping vegetables or being outside in nature. I longed for intellectually stimulating work, deeply enjoying preparing talks, delving into Scripture, and our theology lessons. But outside of those moments, I often felt angry and frustrated. Yet, shame prevented me from expressing my feelings. *I shouldn't feel this way.* My belief in "obedience" silenced me. *I ought to do as you say regardless of what I think or how I feel.* I thought that the sisters had clearly been praying far longer than I have, so they must know more than I do. Living with the same people I worked with also amplified the pressure in a new and unanticipated way. Though I often felt ashamed of my bad moods that did not align with my ideals, I could not run away and hide when I needed a break. I had very little skill with how to handle conflict outside of knowing how to avoid escalating an issue.

After two years in community, I could no longer endure. As I wept at the thought of another painful moment of feeling alienated in community, something within me spoke: *This is not right.* I had reached my breaking point, and I made the painful decision to leave the life I had been convinced was for me. *Maybe I hadn't really discerned my vocation in the first place*, I thought. Looking back, perhaps the healing I needed required a different timeline and care than the community could offer.

During my last retreat before I left, I was captivated by the image of the Eucharist in the tabernacle, its doors swung wide open. The

Eucharist was both inviting me into his home and offering himself with arms extended. In the Eucharist, I understood Jesus saying to me, "I give you all of me. I don't hold anything back; I give you my very own body, to feed you, to sustain you. I want to give myself to you today and every day. I give you all of me. And I am here for you."

At the time, I didn't know what Jesus meant by, "I give you all of me." Yet, I was filled with awe. In that moment when I was terrified of God's judgment and punishment, Jesus, through the Eucharist, responded with words of love and promise. When I was despairing that I was disobeying God by leaving Verbum Dei, Jesus instead showed me how much he gives himself to me, beyond any limits or conditions I placed on his love.

LEAVING VERBUM DEI

Transitioning out of Verbum Dei was a radical ending I did not expect; it felt like a dream shattered. I couldn't understand why something that seemed so right did not work out. I struggled to make sense of what happened. My therapist and other spiritual mentors believed I lacked "freedom" in my vocation. I did not understand what they meant by "freedom." Nor could I shake the conviction that God didn't want me to leave the community. I struggled to know which voice within me to trust. Was God really urging me to return to the community? I had too much resentment and fear in my heart to even consider the possibility. Unable to perceive anything clearly in prayer, God seemed to be silent. I had been unable to hear God during my last retreat in Verbum Dei, likely because I could only focus on my anxious questions regarding what I should do. Perhaps God's voice was being silenced by my own fear of what I didn't want to hear.

I felt a lot of anxiety following my transition out of the community. There was so much I didn't know about my future: *What would I do now? How would I make ends meet? Who would I share my life with?* I knew I could go back to engineering, but I also believed that I would end up in the same place I had been before: unfulfilled. I worked part-time in a biotechnology lab at a community college, and my heart was simply not in the work. I missed ministry. I missed praying in community. During this time, I was fortunate to live two blocks away from a chapel, where I could attend daily Mass. Kneeling before the Eucharist, I begged for consolation, which I often received. It took me some time to understand, but Jesus continued to give of himself to me, as he promised.

JESUS' INVITATION TO GENTLENESS

> Come to me, all you who are weary and are carrying heavy burdens, and I will give you rest. Take my yoke upon you and learn from me; for I am gentle and humble in heart, and you will find rest for your souls. For my yoke is easy, and my burden is light. (Matt 11:28–30)

I discovered this passage from Matthew's Gospel and was deeply intrigued by it. I felt tired and overburdened. What did it mean to have a gentle and humble heart? What did rest look like? What did it mean to take Jesus' yoke upon me?

Working hard, taking advantage of the best opportunities available, and excelling were highly valued by my parents. When I was a child, invitations to play from neighborhood friends were turned down, as my homework was top priority. Requests for help with homework were denied; it was my responsibility alone. Both mistakes and idleness were unacceptable. I grew to be a driven, determined, independent, and highly productive perfectionist, unconsciously seeking to fulfill others' expectations of me. All these skills obtained what both my parents and I intended: academic and career success. Together, we rejoiced in my achievements, and I relished the praise and recognition of others.

After transitioning out of Verbum Dei, I was determined to resist the impulse to fill up my schedule. Instead, I decided to rest. Tentatively moving forward despite not knowing where God was calling me, I registered for the prerequisite courses to realize a different dream of studying theology. I also signed up for voice and yoga classes, both of which I enjoyed, and which offered moments of respite from the anxiety of the transition. I read poetry by mystics and daily reflections by Richard Rohr, exploring new sources of wisdom. Serendipitously, a close friend married shortly after I moved out of the community, and I reconnected with friends and former coworkers. I learned to enjoy simply being. Spending time with friends and loved ones offered me the precious gifts of love and support. My therapist consistently provided me with the essential, safe space in which I could express myself completely. She modeled the compassion I lacked for myself; listening to her insights slowly enabled me to grow into treating myself with compassion. She also continued to affirm that my thoughts, feelings, and opinions mattered, and I began to believe her as I found my voice.

I continued to go to Verbum Dei's prayer groups and retreats; I wanted to remain connected to the community's charism, which had opened so much within me. A long-time lay participant became my spiritual companion; our conversations consoled me and kept me grounded. During the week, I prayed in a patch of grass in a quiet part of my community college's campus, soaking in the warmth of the sun, the bright green of the grass, and the small, white wildflowers. Rather than trying to control my thoughts, seek answers, or focus on Scripture that I could no longer make sense of in my nonreligious life, I would let my mind wander, relaxing into the stillness and solitude. I let go and simply existed. Although I did not perceive God's response with any clarity, I found rest from my anxious thoughts.

I was living the least productive life I had ever led, and yet, God did not punish me. Instead, God continued to bless me through the consolation I received at Mass, through the love and joy in spending time with my friends, and through opening doors to graduate school. While my inertia could have been worrisome, it was my time and space to come to know the unconditional nature of God's love.

WHERE WOULD MY JOY COME FROM?

As I write this, it has been over three years since I transitioned out of Verbum Dei. In that time, I began to study theology at a Jesuit graduate school, moved into a lay intentional community with fellow graduate students, began and ended a serious relationship, and moved back home during the COVID-19 pandemic. Though I stepped through the doors that God opened for me to graduate school, I continued to carry the inner turmoil and confusion mixed with grief, which was heightened by being in a small community of students who were predominantly in religious life. I did not completely understand what happened, nor was I at peace with my transition out of Verbum Dei.

Even though studying theology had been a dream of mine, the reality was much more difficult than I anticipated. In addition to inner turmoil and grief, my insecurities were overwhelming. Academically, I was less prepared than my classmates, the majority of whom came with strong backgrounds in philosophy and theology; my twelve years of study and experience as an engineer were of little use. My spiritual and emotional chaos significantly diminished my ability to focus, and I spent hours with my homework assignments without making much progress. To my dismay, class discussions were the predominant style of teaching rather than lectures, and I felt that I had nothing to contribute. In addition to my academic struggles, I continued to adjust to life without a sizeable paycheck, struggling to cook for myself and to make that a priority. Furthermore, I was surrounded by people in religious life, and I was afraid that I would be judged for my decision to leave or pressured to go back. Throughout my first semester, I often retreated to my room to break down and weep. A member of my living community provided invaluable support, sharing her own struggles with transitioning to graduate theological studies, and reassuring me that things would get better. "You can do it," she insisted. Having overcome her own challenges and making it to her final year of studies herself, she was living proof.

Given my loneliness and my anxiety regarding the uncertainties of my future, meeting someone special felt all the more meaningful and significant. So many things about my boyfriend aligned with what I hoped for in a partner, and I wanted to believe that God had given him to me as my future husband. However, I revealed the true state of my heart as I expressed to God, "I want this relationship, even if you don't." Even though I missed religious life, I resisted and couldn't accept the idea of going back. I dove into the relationship.

My initial excitement gave way to increasing sadness and disturbing but clearer moments of prayer. No matter how much I wanted to be happy, the deepest part of me was becoming increasingly unhappy. After six months of dating, my boyfriend and I attended a silent retreat together, hosted by Verbum Dei. During the retreat, God revealed to both of us in prayer that we were not for each other. A couple of weeks later, I stumbled upon a small poster of Mark 12:30–31, which read: "You shall love the Lord your God with all your heart, and with all your soul, and with all your mind, and with all your strength....You shall love your neighbor as yourself." It was clear to me how far my heart was from resonating with this passage. I had followed myself rather than God, and my selfishness had replaced love.

In my grief and confusion, I wondered, *Where would my joy come from?* I had tried religious life and that hadn't worked out. As much as I wanted to make my life as a layperson work, I couldn't imagine a future in which I was happy. To be true to my deepest self, I had to let my partner go, and with him, my closest friend and spiritual companion. To become more fully the person I am called to be, it was increasingly looking like I needed to let go of my hope of marriage. As much as I wanted it to be otherwise, I felt that I had to come to terms with the pattern that I did not find deep joy or fulfillment but rather increasing sadness and anxiety in partnership. I lost hope. There were glimpses of God breaking through the depression, a voice within reminding me that there was still beauty in life, a presence of someone wrapping their arm around me. But for some time, I did not feel God's presence with me. And yet, God continued to make God's presence known, through the lament songs that would repeatedly play on my Pandora radio and through the kindness and care of friends and family. Powerfully, God met me in prayer on a Saturday morning at Verbum Dei, as I repeatedly implored God with Abraham's words, "Do not pass by your servant" (Gen 18:3). Half an hour of kneeling with my forehead to the ground, begging for God's presence, brought me the deep sense of God's peace and consolation that I yearned for. When the time of prayer was over and it was time to go, I wept. I did not want to leave Verbum Dei's house of prayer, where I felt God's presence so strongly.

Back in graduate school, my lay intentional community provided the autonomy, acceptance, and support I needed to heal and to grow. They were not a judgmental group, which meant a lot because I could not handle judgment at the time. Another roommate's empathy and understanding when I was triggered by my spiritual director's criticism broke through the pain, as she gently held my face to keep me from turning away. Her words, "I love you," allowed me to finally perceive God's own loving words in prayer. The community was where I began to lead prayer again, and their affirmation and support rebuilt my confidence as I rediscovered my joy. From playing games to watching movies, to learning from each other and laughing together, moments of community were precious gifts. While our community was not perfect, my roommates offered their care and emotional support, which meant a great deal to me. Their acts of love, both small and great, contributed to my healing and revivification.

Six months after the breakup, a group of classmates and I went on a class immersion trip to Israel and Palestine. Meditating on and praying with different parts of Jesus' life gave new life to my dead faith. At the garden Catholic tradition holds is the Garden of Gethsemane, I meditated upon Jesus' agony. Though what I feared regarding my own future paled in comparison to the brutality of crucifixion, Jesus' anguish and struggle to accept God's will resonated deeply with mine. I felt invited to remain with Jesus' final assent, "Your will be done." A couple of days later, I was struck by a line from the daily readings, "Keep yourself from idols" (1 John 5:21), which I understood to be God affirming that my desire for a human partner was not what God desired for me. Later in the day at the Mount of Temptation in Jericho, where tradition holds that Jesus was tempted by the devil in the desert, I surrendered my desire to God.

We also met several women leaders of nonprofit organizations dedicated to empowering women with the necessary skills to be able to find employment, as well as to building a community dedicated to peace, equality, and justice among Israelis and Palestinians. In hearing each of the women share the work that they were accomplishing, they reminded me of the kind of person I had once dreamed of being. Intelligent, strong, and determined, they were women dedicated to their missions and passionate about the well-being of others. Their blazing lives lit a small light within me to want such a life again. Though I did not know exactly how such a life for me would take shape, at the Church of the Annunciation in Nazareth, I felt the deepest part of me express to God: *I want to give my whole life to you*. While I did not make any concrete steps or decisions, my prayer reflected a major shift in my relationship with God: a rebuilding of trust and a budding desire to surrender to what God desires for my life.

The final destination in our trip was Galilee, visiting places where Jesus had lived and ministered. I didn't anticipate how much it would mean to me to walk in the same places that Jesus had been. Jesus felt real in a way he had never felt before, and I was filled with awe. Numerous paintings, icons, and mosaics also brought Jesus' ministry to life, especially his healings. Previously, Jesus was primarily a preacher to me, calling people to conversion. Seeing and meditating upon the stories of Jesus healing the sick touched me as I began to notice Jesus' selfless care for the well-being of others. Jesus' healing was not only for the physically ill. I was moved to tears to see that Judas had a place among the disciples in the Church of Magdala, despite his betrayal. Jesus' compassion for others was never so real to me.

Following our immersion trip, I settled more into my life as a graduate student, letting go of the uncertainties surrounding my future and surrendering my hopes for a partner. Regaining my ability to focus,

I delved into my studies. A few months later, the COVID-19 pandemic hit. As prison ministry and summer plans to support a theology program in Spanish for leaders in Latinx ministry moved fully online, I went home to Maryland to be with my family. My search for God, for healing, and for happiness continues in this new context.

Sometimes I look back and wish my path had been a straight trajectory and not muddled by my insecurities. Despite my regrets, I remember a talk I heard by biblical scholar Rev. Dr. Renita J. Weems shortly after the breakup. I recall her sharing her insight that mistakes are the next step a person needs to take in order to move forward. These days I am striving to see my struggles through my prolonged searching for God as a part of my journey to become more fully human.

In the process of becoming fully human I have discovered the depths of God's love. Repeatedly, I have forgotten all that I had experienced of God. Other times, I wanted to give up on seeking God, as God wasn't making any positive difference in my life. I am immeasurably grateful for the people and the graced moments of prayer that have allowed me to finally rediscover God's love, a love that fulfills the deepest needs of my heart. No matter where I have ended up in my journey, God was still with me, giving Godself to me, over and over again, even if it took my heart some time to perceive God's love. As the Psalmist wrote, and I have come to know: "If I make my bed in Sheol, you are there" (Ps 139:8). And in the graced though long and at times painful journey of seeking God once again, letting go of what impedes, I am coming to know God more deeply. Recently praying with Mary's Annunciation, my heart filled with fear at the angel's invitation, and the potential reality that I am called to religious life. Unable to relate to the young and innocent teenage Mary who said, "Yes," I turned to forty-something-year-old Mary, who had witnessed both her son's death and resurrection. I held my fear alongside Mary's experience, and slowly, the fear in my heart dissolved. I was free. Death, sadness, and struggle do not have the final say. I have seen in my own life the slow reemergence of new life. I can say yes to trust again.

NOTES

1. "Who We Are," Verbum Dei USA, accessed November 16, 2021, https://verbumdeiusa.org/who-we-are/.

2. "Our Ministries," Verbum Dei USA, accessed November 16, 2021, https://verbumdeiusa.org/our-ministries/.

3. Verbum Dei's discernment program was an opportunity to develop a prayer life and deepen one's relationship with God, while also participating in Verbum Dei ministries and living in community. It was not necessary for participants to leave their jobs to discern, which is significant for those who are not ready or able to do so. At the time, I lived with two other women who were also discerning, as well as a Verbum Dei sister. The sisters were committed to supporting us in our discernment, regardless of whether one's call was to religious life or not, to Verbum Dei or not. Ultimately, as one of the sisters shared with me, the "goal" of the program wasn't an answer, but to develop a deeper relationship with God.

Chapter 3

LEARNING TO SPEAK THE LANGUAGE OF FEMINISM IN THE SEMINARY CLASSROOM

Stephanie Boccuzzi

DIMINISHING WOMEN'S POWER

Serena Williams was made into a caricature after her loss at the 2018 Australian Open by Mark Knight, a cartoonist from Melbourne's *Herald Sun.*[1] Williams was depicted as a stereotype of an angry black woman with oversized lips and curves. Knight portrayed her as a toddler throwing a tantrum on the tennis world stage, a binky cast aside next to her racket. During this important match, umpire Carlos Ramos believed Williams to have received coaching from her box, and she was docked a point for breaking her racket. Williams then called the umpire a "thief" and was further penalized by a whole game in the championship match. In the caricature, it is also worth pointing out that Williams's opponent is illustrated as a small, white woman with blonde hair. However, her opponent was Naomi Osaka, a Haitian and Japanese player who stands out as an American-born and U.S.-trained athlete who now represents Japan on the women's tour. Osaka is not white, nor does she have blonde hair. Osaka has brown skin and her features reflect the racial combination of her parents' Haitian and Japanese origins. Knight's caricature of both women perpetuates a racist dichotomy that portrays Osaka as white, small, and docile, which sharply contrasts with the portrayal of Williams as angry, large, and out of control. Is this because Osaka behaves "appropriately" during this match and, therefore, conforms to the white standard of acceptable womanly behavior? Does her youth and perceived naiveté on the tennis world stage make it easier for men to lump her into white culture? This is not acceptable, and the abhorrent racism cannot be rationalized away or perceived as inconsequential. It is *very* revelatory in its exposure of explicit bias against darker-skinned female athletes.

It should also be noted that the speech bubble, which surrounds the umpire, Ramos reads, "Can you just let her win?" Mocking the twenty-three-time champion, who set out to break the record of twenty-four Grand Slams won by Margaret Court, the cartoonist made Williams out to be an erratic woman who lost control of herself. During the match, the Spanish umpire, sitting above the court in a position of power, reprimands her actions harshly. When compared to her male counterparts in the sport, Williams's frustration is tame. Footage of Novak Djokovic and the beloved Roger Federer reveal moments of outrage against umpires with the use of language far worse than Williams's reactions, yet they received no penalty. As a Black woman who dominates the sport of tennis, she has revolutionized the game, not just with unprecedented tennis fundamentals, but also with her boundary-pushing fashion on court, her entrepreneurial success, and her outspokenness about issues of justice in the sport and beyond. There is no doubt women are held to a higher standard than men in this sport. As a Black woman, Serena is under even more scrutiny, and her demeanor, emotions, and use of language are quickly judged by male commentators and the media. What appears to men as female anger, outrage, or unprofessional conduct, is just the opposite. It is the rightful expression of athleticism from a world-class athlete. Her success threatens many men. It is easy to judge her and weigh in on how she should be penalized, while at the same time championing the men's game as the standard of true athleticism. Men "battle" and "duke it out," as many commenters explain. Men are not held responsible for their raw emotions but are praised for them. Simply put, in a moment when Serena defied the gaze of what the male imagination believes a dignified female athlete looks like, she lost the ability to define herself and, thus, is caricaturized.

As a collegiate tennis player, I think back on this caricature often. I remember all too well the times on the court when I yelled in moments of frustration and encountered judgment from both opponents and onlookers. Whether the match was won or lost, more often than not, I left the court painfully aware of how I "overreacted." Of course, the men's team who traveled with us was seen as competitive and fighters when they screamed and threw rackets. The double standard here is clear.

Tennis is a solitary sport. In every match, the player experiences a battle with the mind and body. The correlation between mental toughness and technique is remarkable. The onset of emotions, whether good or bad, has a direct effect on performance. Williams is a master of this delicate relationship between mind and body. She is revered as one of the best, if not the best, female tennis player in the history of the game because she is disciplined and never stops working on her mental game, as well as her strokes. In her years of experience, she has defined for herself who she is and what she stands for. Serena is a world champion. She is a mother, a sister, and a friend to many women on the tour. She is a fashion icon, an entrepreneur, and a feminist thinker. Most importantly, for the game of tennis, she is a woman who defies gender norms and confronts racism in order to evolve the game of tennis into the people's game, rather than a game only accessible to the elite. Both Ramos's unfair penalizing of Williams and Knight's racist rendering of the incident are weak attempts to diminish the power of Serena Williams.

LEANING INTO WOMEN'S POWER

Unfortunately, Serena's experience is not isolated within the sport of tennis. More often than not, women in most professions experience unequal treatment and endure inappropriate comments. During my undergraduate studies in business, I was often one of five or six women in a classroom of twenty. As a professor of management pointed out once, women in the classroom submit assignments on time and perform drastically better on assignments when compared to their male counterparts. This professor then noted the correlation between female students' performance in the classroom and the rising number of women in positions of leadership in the corporate world. Interestingly, Sheryl Sandberg's *Lean In* was published in my junior year.[2] Her book was incorporated into our business curriculum and was embraced by male and female faculty alike. In *Lean In*, Sandberg explores gender inequality in the workplace and why women are underrepresented and undervalued in the global workforce. She points out that women are more likely to hold themselves back while their male counterparts unashamedly dive in. For example, she explains that women are far less likely to ask for raises and promotions because they undersell their value and are afraid of being perceived as domineering. This highlights society's unequal expectations regarding the role of women in the workplace and exposes both the conscious and unconscious biases against women who seek positions of leadership. When male counterparts are rewarded and female colleagues are paid less for the same title, Sandberg urges women to lean in as much as they can to challenge the systems of oppression that have kept women from coming to the table. Ultimately, she offers women ways to empower themselves and support one another as they take on deserved positions and leadership roles.

Serena Williams and Sheryl Sandberg would prove useful to me as I entered the seminary classroom. Although they excel in the worlds of tennis and business, these two women are perfect dialogue partners for women who find themselves in theology and ministry. They have helped raise society to new levels of consciousness and have not backed down in the face of opposition. Rather, resistance to their work has only strengthened their efforts to empower women. I call on them now because they were so important to me during my formative years as a young woman, and they remain active agents of change still today.

Prior to beginning graduate studies of theology, I decided to do a yearlong service program in Quito, Ecuador. There I faced a new set of challenges and sought another female role model who could help me digest my experience and inspire me to think about things differently. I did not identify a specific woman as my source of inspiration. Instead, I became inspired by the women with whom I lived in community, who were drawn to service in the same way I was. We all became fast friends as we discovered our shared passion and steadfast commitment to the mission of the Center for Working Families. This *obra social* (community work) accompanies Quito's most vulnerable by offering a wide variety of educational and social assistance programs meant to empower rather than hand out charity. As yearlong volunteers, we were primarily teachers, but we realized we could use our individual gifts to meet some of the other needs presented to us by the families of the Center. As a community of women, we championed each other's ministries and learned to be utterly vulnerable with each other. This sparked a fierce companionship that remains alive today.

During this year of service, I also underwent great personal and spiritual growth. I received great consolation as God continued to reveal Godself to me through the love and hospitality of my students and their families. I was humbled by the abundance of generosity they showed me as I served them. This accompaniment I experienced, by both the women I lived in community with and the families of the Center, enriched my life and drastically reoriented my desires and future aspirations. Toward the end of the year, I found myself in constant prayer with the Holy Spirit as I navigated what my next step would be after leaving Quito.

I grew up in what I call a healthy Catholic household. Our home was, to use the language of Vatican II, a "domestic church."[3] Like many families, we went to weekly Mass and received the sacraments as we grew up. We undoubtedly did our Catholic "duty," but my parents also took special care to incorporate prayer into all facets of our life. We were raised with an understanding that we were a part of the community we lived in, and we were taught to serve this community. We reflected on Scripture as we drove to Mass, and my mom was involved in teaching Sunday school throughout our lives. My father was Jesuit educated and instilled within us the underlying belief that God's love abounds in us and that we are perpetually called into deeper relationship with our Creator. This domestic church gave me the tools to understand myself, as well as my relationship with others and the world. My father and I often spoke of the power of education and the responsibility that comes with that education. My parents raised me to believe that it is through prayer and trust in God that we discern how we can share our gifts freely and abundantly. Therefore, in my discernment process at the end of my volunteer year in Quito, I decided to pursue a Master of Divinity in the fall of 2016. I saw myself working in a faith-based nonprofit and realized this type of work required a new set of tools. With my experience and former studies in hand, I entered graduate studies with a profound sense of clarity and confidence. I wanted to bring to my future career both a solid theological foundation and a mature pastoral sensitivity to serve the people of God as they deserved.

WHO DO I SAY THAT I AM?

I was very naïve when I began the Master of Divinity program. I did not realize I was going to be in the minority as a Catholic woman, and I was very confused as to why people kept calling me a "lay ecclesial minister." Honestly, I had never heard the term before, and I quickly determined that it was not how I wanted to define myself. I had to ask myself if my value or worth change because I was "lay," meaning I was not and could never be ordained. What if I did not want to be an "ecclesial minister"? Did my passion to work outside of the Church structure and institution mean I should not pursue a Master of Divinity? Despite my questions, I was eager to be in the classroom alongside a diverse group of people, including men preparing for ordination, and I wondered what new opportunities for collaboration could look like.

In my first years of study, I counted myself lucky to be studying with supportive peers. My classmates and I slowly worked out what it meant to be in dialogue with each other, and deep friendships formed. I experienced community, as I had at other points in my life, and I grew in gratitude for the opportunity to learn and my choice to pursue the study of theology. Amidst this, though, I became increasingly bothered by the number of times I was also referred to as a "laywoman." The term *ecclesial minster* faded away, and I discovered that my identity as a woman was emphasized more than the potential job title I may or may not have within the Church in the future. I had the sense there was always an underlying division between the ordained or soon-to-be ordained and those who were entirely excluded from ordination. I met my husband in the Master of Divinity program, and we have discussed the difference in the understanding of "layman" compared to "laywoman." To be a "layman" means the man has chosen not to pursue ordination. The option to respond to a vocational call to the deaconate or the priesthood is always open to laymen. In a seminary setting, laymen are invited to discern the call to ordination, even if they have never expressed an interest in ordination. While to be a laywoman in the seminary is to experience a double dismissal. Laywomen are not on the ordination track, nor can they be.

Therefore, to be a woman in the Church means fewer avenues are available for pursuing one's call. I am not discrediting the vocational call to the religious life. In fact, I discerned it and discovered it was not where God was calling me. I have sustained beautiful friendships with women religious, and they have been my spiritual directors, my greatest

---

confidants, and my cheerleaders in moments of doubt and weakness. Women religious have shown me how beautiful my life is as a child of God and empowered me to share the light within me with the world. In graduate studies, I saw limitations placed upon my ability to share that light within me for the first time. I also listened to the community of women around me and heard women speak about their calls to ordination. I was profoundly touched by their stories and shared in their pain.

In our studies, we embraced the concept of the Holy Spirit as the source of inspiration and of God's love at work in the world. We also know the Spirit to be the "advocate" Jesus shared equally with his followers after his death and resurrection. The Holy Spirit's work in the world inspires so many, yet in Divinity school, I realized that despite tradition and our interpretations of Scripture, the clergy could manipulate people's understanding of the Spirit. If the Holy Spirit descended on everyone, why do men get to define what is and is not the Holy Spirit in such a limiting way? I value the important distinctions between ministers and ministries in the Church, but I struggle to understand how the Church hierarchy can place limits on the Spirit's work within the hearts of the people of God. It seems to me an obvious a blatant manipulation of the Spirit of God and a threat to the message of the gospel. I did not like the presumptions being made about how I wanted to work for the Church, given that I was in the divinity program.

LEARNING THE LANGUAGE OF FEMINIST THEOLOGY

Consequently, I felt myself disillusioned about the Church and reconsidered if I was really "fit" for the program. It took time to wrestle with my emotions while I continued with my studies. There were periods of desolation, but with the help of my spiritual director, I was able to revisit what it was that drew me to the school and what *I* desired. My director helped me understand my own freedom in the midst of my pain and uncertainty. He gave me the space to be angry and to wrestle with God. I confronted my frustration with the label "laywoman" and reimagined for myself what my vocation as a free woman in the Church would mean. I leaned on circles of support where I could openly share my doubts and fears with other women and some men in formation who believed in the women's call to ordination. Focused on God, my deepest desires, and community, I felt greater personal resolve to stay in the program and a renewed focus on my studies.

My community encouraged me to begin taking courses with female faculty members, and I was happy to use my electives to explore new areas of study. Almost immediately, I started to feel a sense of grounding in my own life as I explored liberation and feminist theologies, environmental ethics, and issues of race and justice. To be completely honest, I had never encountered women like these professors before. Their preparation for class shone through engaging lectures and well-facilitated classroom discussions. They also found ways to honor different students' experiences and create meaningful assessments. These women challenged me to think differently about myself as a learner and as a woman of faith. It was inspiring to see how they have spent their life's work researching, writing, and dialoguing with others about ways to better grapple with the ambiguities and nuances that are inherent in Catholic theology. They helped me leave behind my own insecurities and they taught me how to be a responsible student of theology and an agent for change in the world.

These women led me into the deep waters of feminist theologies and let me wrestle with the intense relationship that exists between studying academic theology and engaging in ongoing personal theological reflection. I always appreciate the Jesuit Volunteer Corps motto, "Ruined for life," because it reminds me that if I get too comfortable with the world around me, I need to get out into new communities and learn. Discovering feminist theology "ruined" theology for me. As I delved deeper into the different areas of theology, I became more aware of the lack of female voices and the outright absence or exclusion of women in the history of Christian ministry and scholarship. The more I learned, the more I had to return to prayer and sit with what this awakening within me would mean for my future.

During this time, my personal relationship with Jesus intensified. I found comfort praying with Scripture passages in which Jesus was among women and praised them for their faith (Matt 26:7; Luke 8:43–48; John 20:1–18). I also found myself in class with one of the most brilliant professors I had during my graduate studies. Gina Hens-Piazza, my professor of the Old Testament, taught me the power of utilizing methods of biblical interpretation by critically examining our sacred texts and their ongoing role in shaping our tradition and church today. Through Gina's classes, I understood for the first time that the interpretation of Scripture involves more than simply spiritualizing the text. Instead, it means delving into the historical context, reflecting on the sacred text itself, and putting it in conversation with our world today. This way of "doing theology" is a daunting task because it is not only an academic pursuit but also requires self-examination and awareness of what I bring to the study of Scripture. The examples set by these women unlocked the fire within me to take on this task as well, particularly as it pertains to women and vocational calls to ordination.

By my third and final year in the program, I had carefully selected electives that helped form me into a woman of greater confidence in the classroom. I was learning the language of feminist theologians, and it was weaving its way into the fabric of my education. Feminist theology is liberative, inclusive, and grounded in the experience of women. Feminist theology at its best is also attentive to the ways in which poor and oppressed people, and those on the margins have been mistreated or excluded. Elisabeth Schüssler Fiorenza unapologetically writes:

> That we are excluded from defining the world and the meaning of human life and society is an integral part of our oppression. To break the silence and to reclaim the 'power of naming that was stolen from us (Mary Daly)' must therefore become an integral element in our struggle for liberation from patriarchal structures.[4]

These fierce words explain the struggle of women, not just in theology but in the world. It is important to continue to explore the ways women have lost the ability to define their own experiences. It is necessary to discover how women have been pushed aside and hidden in the history of Christianity. We must examine how feminist methods of interpretation are dismissed as "too particular" and their theological lenses irrelevant and unimportant. What is it about women taking ownership of themselves, their work, and their contribution to theology and ministry that is threatening?

While sitting with these questions, I gained a greater appreciation for the ways patriarchal narratives confine and define women, particularly the ways women in the academic discipline of theology and ministry have experienced the harmful power differential that remains untouched by our Church's ecclesiastical hierarchy. Under the control of male authority, women have been excluded from institutional power. Male clergy enjoy the fundamental freedom to follow a vocational call to serve the people of God and to be ordained by the Church. Yet, women who feel that same vocational call are suppressed based on sexist interpretations of Scripture and Tradition.

When studying the history of Christianity, feminist scholars uncover important women who have been hidden at the edges of history. Even further, feminist scholars offer new methods and tools to understand the role of women in the Church throughout time and today. Feminist scholars are sometimes misunderstood as being exclusive of men. However, this is not the case. Instead, they invite all people into this process of rediscovering the gifts of women in our tradition. Yet, one woman cannot speak for all women everywhere. What women can do is speak from their own geographic, ethnic, and racial backgrounds; by doing so, they give voice to their experiences and raise up justice issues in their communities.

I was very lucky to take a Scripture class with the renowned Gospel of John professor, Sandra Schneiders. She was the first woman to be tenured at The Jesuit School of Theology of Santa Clara in Berkeley and helped to establish the first doctorate program in Christian spirituality at The Graduate Theological Union. In her class, I saw how her experiences as a women broke barriers in the field of biblical interpretation. She revealed to me that my perspective as a woman can impact the interpretation of Scripture and Tradition. During a special gathering of women in theology and ministry, Sandra shared what it was like to study in Rome surrounded by male clergy, the obstacles she faced as she researched and studied, and the ways she was supported in her work. Sandra encouraged me as one of a younger generation of women, who are now accepted as students at Catholic theologates, to be bold and say what we needed to say. Sandra Schneiders, Gina Hens-Piazza, and countless other academic women have given me the lens to honor my own experiences, but, more importantly, taught me to create dialogue and prioritize the voices of oppressed and marginalized people.

These feminist lenses reveal how the Spirit is as fully alive in women as it is in men. The "us/them" dichotomy is a false barrier that protects men in positions of power. How can the Church consciously cherry-pick our Sacred Scriptures to substantiate the claim that leadership in the Church is and should be exclusive to men? *Dei Verbum*, the document on revelation from Vatican Council II (1963–1965), speaks to this relationship that exists between the people of God and the teaching function of the Church as it pertains to the interpretation of Scripture. Interpretation is indeed a delicate task that is to be undertaken with utmost care and consideration; it is to be done by both academic and pastoral minds in conversation with the people of God. The Church meditates on the meaning of Scripture to ensure it responds to the signs of the times with regard to lives of the faithful and contemporary social concerns. *Dei Verbum* explains,

> Now what was handed on by the Apostles includes everything which contributes toward the holiness of life and increase in faith of the peoples of God; and so the Church, in her teaching, life and worship, perpetuates and hands on to all generations all that she herself is, all that she believes. This tradition, which comes from the Apostles, develops in the Church with the help of the Holy Spirit. For there is a growth in the understanding of the realities and the words which have been handed down. This happens through the contemplation and study made by believers, who treasure these things in their hearts (see Luke, 2:19, 51)....For as the centuries succeed one another, the Church constantly moves forward toward the fullness of divine truth until the words of God reach their complete fulfillment in her.[5]

The tradition of the Church has developed over time. The Church is called to constantly move forward in response to the signs of the times. Now, in these times, the Church needs to grapple with feminist approaches to interpretation and continue to develop tradition in a way that includes the experience of women.

AN INVITATION TO MY BROTHERS

In the final semester of my time in graduate school, I chose to take a class entitled "Racializing Jesus." I loved this class, our community of learners, and our ability to dialogue about the challenging task of racializing Jesus. We moved through studying Jesus as an apocalyptic prophet, the complexities of the quest for the historical Jesus, as well as the history of Western biblical interpretation, particularly in Nazi Germany. This then led us to examine critical race theory and the implications of the white Jesus on marginalized ethnic communities today. Most importantly, we spent time examining the historical, cultural, societal, and theological intersections of the Black Christ, *el Cristo Migrante*, and the Asian Jesus. It was not until the very last class in the semester that we broached the topic of feminist Christologies. I have found this relegation of women's perspectives to the end to be a common occurrence throughout my coursework in my MDiv program. In nearly every class that covered feminist criticism, exploring feminist criticism was delayed until one of the last classes of the semester. It often felt like feminist criticism was a "token" method tacked onto the end to check the box of inclusivity. I could not help but feel that consideration of the woman's perspective was an afterthought or, worse, positioned as an obligation rather than a real consideration.

In this final class of Racializing Jesus, in which we finally discussed feminist perspectives, our professor opened the conversation by asking for our initial impressions of an essay in *The Blackwell Companion to Jesus* written by Lisa Isherwood titled "Feminist Christologies."[6] In the assigned reading, Isherwood maps different feminist theologies and points to both their particularities and commonalities. She does an excellent job of providing a selection of the important voices in contemporary feminist Christologies and how they bear on our understanding of the salvation of women. She suggests, "Feminist theologians should seek to destabilize the center by speaking both the language of our intellectual theological fathers and the dialects of our feminist sisters."[7] Sitting in class with this line highlighted and underlined a few times, I kept it in my back pocket to bring out when the time was right. I was excited and ready for this conversation. I was curious to discover my eleven male colleagues' reactions to the text. I also wondered if the one other woman in the class and I would have to carry the conversation.

Silence filled the classroom. As I scanned the room, I saw an increasing number of eyes on me. Not unfamiliar with this feeling, I desperately wished that, just this once, a male colleague would jump in to start the conversation. I was hopeful when a male classmate did speak up, but unfortunately, there was no interrogation of the topic at hand but rather a sheepish "pass off" to me because I was the "resident woman" in the class who could speak to the experience of all women, everywhere. Centering myself, I took a moment to ask the Holy Spirit to inspire my words and give me the patience to engage in dialogue with my brothers about the important work of feminist theologians. I began by reminding my classmates to consider how women relate to Jesus, the man who once walked on earth, and the Christ, the Word made flesh, who came for the salvation of all. I attempted to delicately explain that androcentric Christology is deeply fused into our understanding of Christianity, and that we would be irresponsible students of theology if we did not name this reality. Furthermore, just as we employ methods of liberation to the situation of poor people in Latin America and post-colonial approaches to biblical interpretation, we must investigate the oppression of women and the exclusion of their experience, in church practice and theological reflection.[8]

Silence, again, descended upon the classroom. I was satisfied with the articulation of my thoughts. My fellow female colleague articulated her position, supporting what I had said. I appreciated her boldness when she said, "You know, professor, and no offense, but we did save feminist criticism for the last class. At this point we are somewhat checked-out of the semester, and I am sure not everyone has done this reading." I subtly nodded my head in agreement and scanned the room again to assess the expressions of my male colleagues. I felt tension and loved it. The professor acknowledged the consequences of the order of the syllabus and confessed that he made special efforts in his doctoral studies to take courses solely devoted to feminist perspectives. I appreciated how he owned this oversight but, yet again, silence permeated the classroom. I lingered in the quiet, waiting for a male voice to chime in. Again, no such luck. I raised my hand and said,

> Any good feminist theology is creation-based. It grounds itself in the incorporation of *all* of creation and, of course, uplifts the experiences of women, but in doing so does *not* set out to throw away the history of Christianity or supersede the experience of men. Feminist criticism needs to be carefully studied by men in positions of power. We absolutely need to listen to the voices of women and name the places they have been silenced or forgotten, but it is equally as important that you, my male colleagues, articulate this for yourselves.

Silence ensued. I decided it was time to sit in that silence and allow it to do the talking. Silence causes discomfort. For the two of us women in that classroom it was important to not fill the gaps in the hopes of "getting through." That long moment of silence is indicative of the current environment for women in theology and ministry. Silence can say more than conversation. It can reveal that students have not done the assigned readings, it can hold the space for powerful moments of revelation, and it can expose what is hard to grasp, as well as what needs to be revisited. However, it can also reveal what has been overlooked or what would rather be left untouched by the majority of the people in the classroom. After class that day, I began racking my brain and searching for a way to entice my male colleagues to explore for themselves the task of feminist theologies. Allowing them to evade the task and signal their unwillingness to discuss and engage with pacifying nods was insufficient. Upon reflection, I believe there is a fitting analogy for us women who find ourselves excited by the promise of feminist theology but also frustrated in a lack of expressed appreciation from our community who don't recognize what it can offer our tradition.

When learning a new language, people begin to acquire it by listening and reading first, then by writing and speaking. These receptive skills of listening and reading become productive skills later. The more people hear and read a language, the better they become at writing and speaking it for themselves. True acquisition of another language requires people to construct a sentence based on what *they* have learned, not merely memorizing what they read in a book or repeating what they heard someone else say. If people want to speak in Spanish, they have to search for the right words to construct what they want to say. This takes practice and patience. When living in Ecuador, I underwent this process all day, every day until I became fluent. As I began graduate studies, I experienced this same process in the classroom from my female professors. First, I listened and read about feminist methods extensively before I internalized and claimed them for myself in my speaking and writing. It is my hope for my male colleagues that they will come to see the value of considering women's perspectives. It cannot be the job of women to fill the gaps for men. Instead, men must become active participants in learning the language of feminist theologies. While my male classmates do engage with feminist theology insofar as they read and listen, they rarely grapple with it in their own words. They need to endeavor to articulate these concepts themselves and try this new language out on their own tongues. What better place to do that than in the classroom? I believe it is the role of professors and students alike to prioritize learning languages different from our own so that we can be in solidarity with one another. If feminist approaches to theology remain only an afterthought, the patriarchal narrative will continue to be the default language with which we articulate our faith tradition.

In learning the language of theology, I also had to learn how to unlock my imagination and open myself up to the mysteries of faith. In my Racializing Jesus class, I discovered how to suspend my own comfort with the white Christ in order to authentically imagine the implications and revelatory power the Black Christ, for example, offers. My male counterparts may have been "giving me the floor" in order to learn from my perspective. However, when I thought about our other conversations pertaining to different representations of Jesus, I realized that the entire class "shared the floor." There were Latino, Black, White, and Asian, queer and straight students in the classroom. At no other point in the semester did we rely on the voices of one minority group, such as the Latino students, for example, when speaking to *el Cristo Migrante* (the Migrant Christ). It was quite the opposite. Many of us loved the lively dialogue that would ensue after student presentations about different representations of Jesus. I find it alarming that when we shifted from investigating the different racial representations of Jesus to studying the feminine Jesus, silence reigned in the room. Isherwood claims that women's oppression is woven into the tapestry of Christianity, and this oppression was on display in our classroom. Unlike in recent history, women are present in some Catholic theologates and contribute their gifts to the academic discipline of theology and ministry alongside men in formation. Despite these women's presence, feminist methods of investigation remain unpursued or ignored by many men. The silence in Racializing Jesus ironically demonstrated the very dynamic Isherwood attempted to expose in her chapter. When the professor created an environment in which Jesus and feminism were in dialogue, gender became a roadblock to our class discussion. I wonder what would have happened if we had allowed ourselves to truly imagine the implications of the feminine Jesus. What type of encounter would have awaited us? I know that conversation would have been communal and prophetic. There could have been dialogue about what makes the feminine Jesus so uncomfortable for so many. Yet, unfortunately, we were not able to explore that potential revelatory conversation because the feminine Jesus is evidently so intimidating and such an unfamiliar concept that it remained out of reach.

HEAR THE WOMEN

Despite my frustrations with this particular class, I did find hope in my sacred texts class. First, turning to well-known women in Scripture, I learned to reconsider their role in salvation history, rather than passively accepting them as simply supporting actresses to flashy male protagonists. My professor, Gina Hens-Piazza, invited me to examine what female minor characters reveal despite the fact that they have been "read past" and oftentimes misunderstood.[9] This process of reclaiming the experience of women in Scripture was a thrilling process of discovery that I eagerly consumed. Employing a method that allows for carefully searching through texts in order to uncover the bold presence of women within our scriptural tradition remains a source of nourishment for me in my current ministry and in my personal prayer. It is also something I now encourage women to do for themselves because I have discovered its transformative power through my own experiences. Reclaiming and renaming these women is a simple and effective exercise. For example, women might ask the following:

- What if the Exodus story is not only about Moses but also about Miriam and the Hebrew midwives, Shiphrah and Puah, who changed the fortunes of Israel (Exod 1:15; 2:10)?
- What if the unnamed Levite concubine is not remembered as a slave to male desire and a victim of violence? What if she is reclaimed as Our Suffering Sister and venerated for her courageous choice to leave her husband and return to her ancestral home (Judg 19:27–29)? Furthermore, what if Our Suffering Sister is not isolated within the horror found in Judges? What if she is set free by the story of women's cooperation for the sake of survival in the narrative about Ruth and Naomi that follows (Ruth 1:15–18)?
- Turning to the New Testament, what if Mary Magdalene is not a sinful prostitute but the Herald of the Good News of the Risen Christ, as she is actually portrayed in all four Gospels (Matt 28:1–10; Mark 16:1–10; Luke 24:1–12; John 20:1–18)?
- What if the Woman with the Hemorrhage is called the Daring Daughter of Sarah? What if this Daring Daughter of Sarah is recognized as exercising her own agency when she touches the cloak of Jesus and draws power out of him? Jesus immediately reincorporates her back into the community, acknowledging her boldness in the face of the disciples' skepticism (Matt 9:20–22; Mark 5:25–34; Luke 8:43–48).
- Finally, what if the Crippled Woman who was bent over for eighteen years becomes the Woman Who Glorified

the Lord by her Life? This woman is worthy of a miracle, and after she is healed, she "began praising God" in the face of the outrage of the leaders of the synagogue (Luke 13:10–17).

These women have often been named by their ailments by male interpreters. What if interpreters of Scripture instead identify these women by their acts of agency and their faith instead of their frailties? By stripping away the titles assigned to them by predominately white, male interpreters, their stories gain new meaning. By engaging in this process, women interpreters articulate the contribution of the women within these texts to the inspired Word of God and revelation. In doing so, these fresh interpretations not only free them, but liberate all women.

Women in community with other women are powerful. Something generative happens when women come together and share their lived experiences with one other. I love the idea that the women of Scripture are women we seek to be in dialogue with today because their witness informs both our self- and collective understanding. When our male colleagues continue to label women from their positions of power within the hierarchy of the Church, how will they be able to preach about women in their homilies? How will they avoid obfuscating the gifts of women and limiting their agency? Voices have been silenced. Women have been erased from history. Women's lives are limited and controlled as they are defined and judged by their bodies. Patriarchal notions of sexuality and sin are projected onto the female form. Women are reduced to virgin, bride, whore, or diseased, and are blatantly objectified. This is why it is so important for women to be present in Catholic theologates. How are male seminarians, who are silent when the focus of the class is women, going to be able to respond to half of the needs of the people of God? How can clergy minister to people whom they reduce to the categories of virgin, bride, and so on? Despite the ways women can be caricaturized as disturbances to the status quo of the classroom, women have a responsibility to one another and to God herself to sincerely and loving invite others into our process of naming and reclaiming. When I find myself in strained situations in my ministry or in the classroom, I know I am in good company. I experience liberation as I wrestle with the injustices I witness because I know I am not alone. Our struggles are made holy by the power of being in community with one another. Collective encounter, grounded in fidelity and love of Tradition, produces a reclamation of our place in Tradition and glorifies God.

I want all women to feel empowered and believe they are equal partners in theology and ministry. Women are preachers of the good news, well-equipped theologians, and leaders in the Church. To quote the fearsome Ruth Bader Ginsburg: "Women belong in all places where decisions are made." God invites women to transform the injustices they face. I find inspiration in Saint Paul, who insisted that the gifts of Spirit manifest differently within each person (1 Cor 12). To be true followers of Jesus Christ, women must share their gifts freely with one another in order to strengthen the whole community. Jesus proclaims many times, "The Kingdom of God is at hand!" (Matt 3:2; Matt 4:17; Mark 1:5; Luke 10:9). This kingdom is here and happening right now. There is urgency to live as God commands us. We are given the invitation to love and honor all creation—male and female. This is what makes an examination of our institutional church so critical and timely. Jesus' ministry was not passive but incredibly proactive. He directly challenged authority and modeled that for us. As a woman of faith who operates within an exclusive and patriarchal system of leadership, I take comfort in Jesus' rebellion against authorities. This very call we have as women to be equal participants in the Church is outrageously Christian. Saint Paul, the saints and martyrs, and the history of our church reveal the radical faith it takes to be a follower of Jesus and the consequences, good and bad, that flow from it; yet, today when we call for women's equal participation in the Church we are ignored, cast aside, and wrapped up in canonical paperwork. Even still, we rally and come together. As women we know the free work of the Spirit in the world ignites our imaginations and God's generative love in the world through us.

Therefore, I return to the label given to me at the start of my graduate studies in the Master of Divinity program. I say with great clarity and certainty that I am not a "laywoman," dismissed and categorized by my supposed inability to be ordained. I will not define myself based on what I am not. Instead, I reclaim the power to name who I am in relationship to the world and to God, the Creator. I am a missionary and apostle of Jesus Christ. I am teacher and a preacher of the Word of God. I am a minister to the marginalized people of New York City. Above all, I am a woman who loves God.

NOTES

1. "Herald Sun Backs Mark Knight's Cartoon on Serena Williams," *Herald Sun*, September 12, 2018, https://www.heraldsun.com.au/news/victoria/herald-sun-backs-mark-knights-cartoon-on-serena-williams/news-story/30c877e3937a510d64609d89ac521d9f.

2. Sheryl Sandberg, *Lean In: Women, Work, and the Will to Lean* (New York: Alfred A. Knopf, 2013).

3. Paul VI, *Lumen Gentium*, The Dogmatic Constitution on the Church, November 21, 1964, Vatican website, https://www.vatican.va/archive/hist_councils/ii_vatican_council/documents/vat-ii_const_19641121_lumen-gentium_en.html, no. 11.

4. Elisabeth Schüssler Fiorenza and Mary Collins, eds., *Women Invisible in Church and Theology*, Concilium 182 (December 1, 1985), 9–10.

5. Paul VI, *Dei Verbum*, Dogmatic Constitution on Divine Revelation, November 18, 1965, Vatican website, https://www.vatican.va/archive/hist_councils/ii_vatican_council/documents/vat-ii_const_19651118_dei-verbum_en.html, no. 8.

6. Delbert Burkett, ed., *The Blackwell Companion to Jesus: Burkett/ The Blackwell Companion to Jesus* (Oxford, UK: Wiley-Blackwell, 2010), accessed July 19, 2020, http://doi.wiley.com/10.1002/9781444327946.

7. Lisa Isherwood, *Introducing Feminist Christologies*, The Blackwell Companion to Jesus (Oxford, UK: Wiley-Blackwell, 2002), 432.

8. Isherwood, *Introducing Feminist Christologies*, 427.

9. Gina Hens-Piazza, "Women: Nameless, Foreign, Misjudged, Questionable" lecture in course Children of Sarah, Hagar, and Mary, November 8, 2017, Jesuit School of Theology of Santa Clara University, Berkeley, California.

Chapter 4

CHALLENGING THE **FOCUS** NARRATIVE OF EVANGELIZATION FOR THE SAKE OF MARGINALIZED STUDENTS

Mary Perez

The communal kitchen was one of my favorite spaces in the campus ministry center. Brief chats with students while making tea often developed into longer lunch conversations about friends or family or campus jobs. The informal space of the kitchen provided relaxed moments of encounter where I was privileged to receive stories of success as well as pain. These stories revealed the determination and creativity of first-generation students, the wounds of racialized microaggressions endured by students of color, and the harmful self-doubt perpetuated by "model minority" myths. In the kitchen, I learned the value of a Catholic campus ministry center as a safe haven for students racialized, classified, and categorized as "other" through the social systems, institutional structures, interpersonal relations, and academic expectations of university life.

As a campus minister at the University Catholic Center at the University of California, Los Angeles, in the 2018–19 school year, I had the privilege of accompanying students in their processes of making meaning of their college experience. I loved the diverse expressions of Catholicism that students brought with them into the Center. Devotions to Our Lady of Guadalupe, celebrations of Lunar New Year, and communal dinner nights featuring Filipino or Vietnamese food revealed the expansive racial and ethnic diversity of our students. I loved that our center reflected the American Catholic Church—the Body of Christ that is Latinx, Vietnamese, Korean, Filipino, Black, Italian, German, and more. As a woman of color of Latinx, Filipino, and European decent, I delighted in this space that held many students, particularly the first-generation students of color who shared how their faith kept them connected to their families when so many parts of the college experience created distance between their lived realities and those of their families.

A NARROW **FOCUS**

During this year of campus ministry, I also was introduced to the evangelizing organization FOCUS (Fellowship of Catholic University Students).[1] I was struck by the zeal of the FOCUS missionaries for developing relationships with students and their enthusiasm for fulfilling FOCUS's mission.[2] FOCUS missionaries are an integral part of the Center's life, always in attendance at liturgies and the Center's various social and faith-formational programs. I saw that through FOCUS-led Bible studies, one-on-one relationships (known as "discipling" in FOCUS parlance), and social gatherings, FOCUS missionaries demonstrated their commitment to "inspiring and equipping [students] for a lifetime of Christ-centered evangelization, discipleship, and friendships."[3]

As I came to know more about FOCUS through its materials, the five-day SEEK19 conference, and my interactions and observations of the missionaries on two campuses in Southern California, I saw many benefits and possibilities for deep spiritual growth for students and missionaries. The emphases on relationships, devotion, commitment, community, and learning all spoke to the reality of being a young person trying to navigate faith and the realities of daily life. I witnessed young adult missionaries excitedly sharing their stories of growing in faith and engaging with more intention in Catholic prayer practices.

These practices seemed to center around Mass attendance, adoration, and reading apologetic texts as ways to deepen their faith. Their enthusiasm invited students' participation in both FOCUS programming and campus ministry events. The FOCUS missionaries' regular routines of communal and individual prayer struck me as beautiful examples of their dedication to cultivating interior relationships with Christ. I often saw students join missionaries at daily and Sunday Mass. In conversation with students who participated in discipling with missionaries, I heard stories of newfound attention to relationship with God, self, and church.

But I also found myself troubled by the ways that I was seeing Catholicism portrayed by FOCUS. I was confused by what seemed to me to be limited expressions of who counted as Catholic. The ethnically diverse devotional practices of my students were not the devotional practices that FOCUS elevated as essential to Catholic worship. Devotions to Our Lady of Lavang among Vietnamese students or Our Lady of Naju among Korean students were glossed over and neglected rather than celebrated. The socioeconomic concerns of the first-generation students of color were not mirrored in the narratives FOCUS offered regarding the challenges faced by college students.[4] While FOCUS materials reference being "comfortable in the Jacuzzi,"[5] many students faced other issues, such as needing to provide childcare to younger siblings or translation for parents; they faced circumstances that became potential roadblocks to their education, such as being unable to pay for textbooks because of unexpected expenses like car repair. I often found myself frustrated by what felt like a slice of Catholicism—a manifestation of a white, middle-class American Catholicism—being served as a universal expression of the faith.

As much as I loved the Center at UCLA and the space that it provided for community building and support of students' exploration of their Catholic faith, I realized that the Center, and campus ministry in general, could foster harmful spaces and narratives. I began to wonder: How can campus ministries be best equipped to recognize, celebrate, and support first-gen, BIPOC, and queer students? How can Catholic college campus ministries attend to diverse experiences of Catholicism beyond a singular, narrow definition of Catholicism put forth by FOCUS? How can campus ministers make sure campus ministry is a truly welcoming space that does not negate students' experiences?

I fear that the increasing presence and power of FOCUS will obscure the significant role campus ministries can and should play for all students, particularly BIPOC students. I am concerned that FOCUS's narrative of discipleship perpetuates a Catholicism marked only by the experiences and concerns of cisgender, heteronormative, white middle-class Americans. This fosters a dominant narrative that aims at universality but falls short in attending to the diverse experiences and lived realities of students outside of this dominant white, middle-class identity. My concern is that FOCUS's universalized understanding of Catholicism functions as a project of marginalization, failing to seek the equity and racial justice that are desperately needed in the Catholic Church.

CONSTRUCTING NARRATIVES

What does it mean to be Catholic? Catholic identity has been a buzzword among Catholic individuals and institutions for many years, but what does claiming a Catholic identity entail? What is it that makes a person Catholic? Are there essential characteristics, beliefs, or practices held by Catholics? Is the core of Catholicism the visible practices and rituals that Catholics participate in, such as going to Mass, receiving the sacraments, praying the rosary, or refraining from eating meat on Fridays during Lent? Does claiming a Catholic identity mean I hold particular creedal statements to be true? Does identifying as a Catholic mean that I pass a political litmus test of opposing abortion or embracing social justice? People's responses to what it means to claim a Catholic identity vary widely.

Rather than place value judgments on "right" or "wrong" beliefs or practices within Catholicism, I have come to see the importance of seeking to understand how people make sense of their Catholic identity. Through nine years of teaching in Catholic middle and high schools, I learned that students' lived experiences and relationships with family, friends, teachers, and significant others are critical sites for their theologizing and meaning making. As a scholar in the study of religion, I recognize that the stories people construct around their religious beliefs and practices shape their identities. Therefore, asking questions about how people actively build, foster, and display Catholic identity is a useful enterprise. Given the variety of identifications people hold within Catholicism, based on their race, ethnicity, sexuality, socioeconomic status, or abilities, I've found it fruitful to pay attention to internal diversity within Catholicism. This move has helped me shift from a desire to determine what is right or wrong to a stance of curiosity and listening.[6]

In order to better understand how people make sense of their religious identities, it is helpful to pay attention to the stories that people or groups tell about their faith experiences. These narratives are a way for people to organize their various experiences of Catholicism and decide what it means to them. This process of organizing meaning and experience through the constructive of narratives is not neutral. Narratives do not simply exist in the world, independent and objective. Instead, the narratives people create as they make sense of the world and their religious experiences are made up of particular experiences in their lives, which may differ from the experiences of other believers.

I find this framing helpful for looking at self-narratives and communal narratives. Self-narratives are the stories people use for making meaning of their life experiences. Communal narratives are the stories people develop together as groups or as a society in order to make meaning of collective experiences. Through the process of crafting these self- and communal narratives, people construct their identities, create a sense of belonging, and determine where they locate themselves in relation to others. The ways in which people narrate their individual identities can fluctuate depending on context. For example, I recognize that how I narrate my life (to myself and to others) draws most prominently from my experiences, my family stories, my academic studies, and my Catholicism. Within each of these, I have multiple entry points into telling my story. At times, I encounter my identity as it is shaped in relationship to others and how I understand others' perception of me. This includes societal perceptions.

This leads me to consider the communal narrative of Catholicism developed by FOCUS, as well as the individual narratives of those connected to the organization—campus ministers, missionaries, and students. Before considering the individual and collective impact of FOCUS, we must consider the narrative of Catholicism that FOCUS promotes. The FOCUS narrative reveals its understanding of theology, as well as Catholicism's relationship to society. Rather than a theological or an apologetic conversation with FOCUS materials, a "narrative" approach considers the building blocks of Catholic experiences that FOCUS uses to construct its organization's narrative. Placing an emphasis on a variety of sources from which FOCUS tells its story of U.S. Catholicism allows campus ministers, FOCUS missionaries, and students to notice whose experiences are included in its story of what it means to be Catholic. This process also calls attention to the experiences that are not reflected in FOCUS's narrative regarding Catholic identity. This allows all those involved in campus ministry to notice and consider the narrative FOCUS constructs in order to help us better respond to the spiritual needs of all Catholics.

Meet Sylvia

The need and desire to belong is at the core of these questions of identity. College students, as young adults navigating new and unfamiliar contexts, are particularly vulnerable as they seek a sense of belonging. It is important to honor the lived experiences of missionaries and students who encounter and make meaning with the FOCUS narrative. I have constructed a narrative of a college student, "Sylvia," who represents an amalgamation of different conversations and stories I encountered in my time as a campus minister. Sylvia helps to bring out elements of students' experience that are important to honor, especially when they are not centered in the narrative of Catholic identity offered by FOCUS. By privileging Sylvia's story and reading it alongside the narrow, universal portrayal of Catholicism FOCUS offers, I highlight the need for campus ministry to promote Catholic narratives that respond to the needs of all students.

FOCUS AND "DYNAMIC, TRANSFORMATIVE DISCIPLESHIP"

When I first learned of FOCUS missionaries and the "dynamic, transformative discipleship"[7] they promote, I was intrigued. I found myself reflecting on the following: How do FOCUS missionaries enact this discipleship? How is it similar to (or different from) my own sense of discipleship? What story fuels FOCUS's image of discipleship?

I begin to look more closely at the image of discipleship in FOCUS by reflecting on my own experience. It's Winter Quarter 2019. I'm remembering how I felt as an undergrad during Winter Quarter: rushed and stressed. Although that was fifteen years ago, the memories of the seemingly never-ending midterms send tingles of anxiety through my stomach. As I chat with a group of sophomores after Sunday Mass, I wonder about how they cope with that anxiety. I return from my thoughts to the excited conversation at hand. This group of four women are recounting their favorite moments from SEEK19. One speaks, with a sense of awe, about the thousands of college students in attendance: "It felt like a sea of people, and it was quite impressive to see that many young people in Mass and at adoration." Another student shared about a talk she attended in which a woman shared her personal conversion story: "She was amazing! Her story was powerful! She went from such trouble and difficulties to being a Catholic mother. Secular culture is so harmful."

"Yeah," the third chimed in, "Choose faith. Resist the temptations of the world." They all nod in agreement and the conversation quickly turns to brunch awaiting them in the dining hall.

The fourth student, Sylvia, who hadn't spoken during this sharing of SEEK stories, lingers as they make their way toward the door. She says quietly that she'd like to come chat with me this week. I smile reassuringly and tell her that I'll send her an email to set up a time. As they walk out, I scan my memories of the conference just three weeks prior in Indianapolis and bring forth a conversation with Sylvia at dinner one night of the conference. She chatted about how glad she was to be there even though it had been a financial stretch for her to make it happen. Missing work for a few days matters when she has books to buy and tuition to pay. Although she was quiet today, she seemed to appreciate attending the SEEK conference.

The SEEK conference is a major part of the FOCUS programming, and it takes place every two years. The missionaries on campus talk about it and advertise it from the start of the school year. "It is life-changing," they eagerly explain. SEEK conferences are an opportunity for students to be thoroughly immersed in the understanding of Catholicism FOCUS promotes. SEEK presents young adults with a framework of Catholicism that offers a clear answer for every situation. Favored practices are repackaged for a millennial audience. Kate Dugan describes SEEK 2013:

Devotion to a hip, young, attractive saint provided a role model of how to negotiate cultural and religious norms. Latin prayer marked and policed the boundaries of this exceptional community, while adoration with confession expected a shared, dramatic experience of God to become a daily relationship with God and a bond with thousands of other millennial Catholics. Through these Catholic prayers, FOCUS taught, modeled, and invited thousands of emerging adults to embody their vision of a dynamically orthodox Catholic community.[8]

FOCUS offers its own unique interpretation of missionary discipleship, as well as a distinctive method of engaging in evangelization. Kate Dugan further summarizes their approach as she says, "FOCUS missionaries keep the ideals of Catholic orthodoxy and culturally savvy dynamism in creative tension as they embody and teach Catholic identity. This is not their grandparents' Catholicism. This is Catholic identity reshaped, remixed, and re-presented for and by millennials."[9] FOCUS aims to make Catholicism relevant to younger generations. Yet is FOCUS's approach relevant to only some? Are some young people left out?

Back in my office, Sylvia reveals her confusion about the SEEK experience, "I kept waiting for something to happen. It seemed like everyone around me felt something new. But I didn't. Is something wrong with me?" She continues, "I feel like I should experience this newness, but I don't. I mean, I love Jesus, I always have, since I was little and prayed to La Virgen while making tamales with my abuelita for whoever among our neighbors might be struggling this month. Do I not love Jesus enough? Why was I the only one who didn't feel something new?"

FOCUS missionaries "disciple" students through a model of "Win-Build-Send," that is, they seek to "win the hearts of college students, build them up in the faith, and send them out into the world."[10] The end goals include sharing the joy of the gospel and living out Jesus' commission to make disciples of all nations (Matt 28:19). For example, to "win" students, missionaries are given a narrative of what needs to be lost, namely that which is "secular" and today's "culture." The "secular" and "culture" are demonized in order to perpetuate the narrative that enables "winning." This message did not resonate with Sylvia. She didn't need to be "won," as she already possesses an integrated faith life. Sylvia's experience is complicated further by the suggestion that "culture" is something negative to be avoided.

FOCUS materials situate students with an essentialized "culture" that employs "secular" as a catchall for ills that must be confronted. As the FOCUS website notes in an introduction to the method of discipleship that FOCUS employs: "We live in a culture that is increasingly hostile to Christianity. Almost everywhere we turn, we are bombarded with a secular outlook on life: in the shows we watch, in the music we listen to, in our schools, in our workplaces and with our peers."[11] This narrative creates a universal "we" who experiences a monolithic cultural context that is antagonistic to Christianity. This binary of secular versus Christianity is perpetuated throughout FOCUS materials to diagnose the cause of problems that college students face and provide motivation for following the path prescribed by FOCUS for being a missionary disciple. Perhaps it is not the intention, yet FOCUS theology effectively erases the unique experiences of individual Catholics who do not fit into its narrative framework.

In an online article entitled "Introduction: Transformative Discipleship," FOCUS describes one person's actions resisting Nazism in Poland in the 1940s as an example of an ordinary person who changed the world by remaining steadfast in his faith.[12] FOCUS then equates the persecution of Catholics by the Nazis to "the culture" we live in today as being "hostile to Christianity." This false equivalency between today's "culture" and Nazi occupation fosters "us vs. them" thinking and cultivates a feeling of victimization. It is problematic that us vs. them thinking and victimization are used as the basis of motivation for discipleship.

Thus, students are encouraged to feel victimized by the "secular" or by the "culture." I am also concerned that the effect of promoting a sense of victimization among young Catholics leads people to believe that they are the ones who are oppressed. If FOCUS invites Catholics to fixate on their own "oppression," then are they absolved from examining the ways that they might be oppressing others? Furthermore, FOCUS teaches students that they experience their own conversion by turning away from this oppressive "culture." However, culture is never clearly defined; it is "secular," it's pervasive, and it's in the movies and on social media. FOCUS also demonstrates no awareness of the white, middle-class *culture* it promotes. The lack of clarity around culture and the vague sense that it is somehow "bad" is also complicated by Sylvia's likely experiences of having been viewed as a cultural other. This is understandably confusing for Sylvia.

> Sylvia: "I also feel like I don't fit in with this group. They think that partying is bad, but I've enjoyed the parties I've gone to. I mean, I'm not going all the time. My service organization went dancing with another group and it was a lot of fun. Am I doing something wrong? Does this mean that I'm not Catholic enough?"

Stories like Sylvia's remind me of students looking for belonging. Students need to feel validated for who they are. They do not need disapproval or a sense that they require conversion from who they have been or from the fears and ills around them. This a different ministerial approach than that of FOCUS, where the appeal of Catholicism is contingent upon demonizing the secular and the other. This tells students that secular is bad, Catholicism is good, but fails to provide them with why exactly and what exactly is bad about it. Nor does it provide a firm footing on what is good.

So far, FOCUS's portrayal of Catholicism does not resonate with Sylvia. She does not understand why her experience differs from her peers. Sylvia came to college with an active faith life that is integrated with her service to others. She "failed" to have a "new" experience of Jesus because her faith likely surpasses the fledgling faith of her friends. Sylvia also "parties" on occasion with her service organization. She lacks the financial resources or the time to party regularly. The highlight of partying for her is the dancing. To paint her experiences of partying with the same brush as those who drink to excess every weekend adds to Sylvia's confusion. Furthermore, Sylvia does not need a conversion experience to turn away from the sinful secular culture. Rejecting culture is dissonant for Sylvia because her culture and faith life are deeply intertwined. Sylvia makes healthier choices than many of her peers and has developed an active faith life. Yet, she is second-guessing herself because she does not fit into the simplistic and dichotomous discipleship that FOCUS enthusiastically promotes.

The binaries created by FOCUS are still more damaging for Sylvia and students like her. When discipleship is reduced to an us vs. them dichotomy, and Sylvia does not clearly fit into the "us" category with her peers who embrace the FOCUS narrative, Sylvia is in danger of being treated as the other. If there is no room for difference within FOCUS's construction of Catholicism, Sylvia, who likes dancing at parties, who *should not* reject her sense of culture, whose prayer experiences differ from her peers, may be vilified or sacrificed at the feet of the FOCUS hegemony.

Furthermore, FOCUS theology does not name its complicity in structures or systems of power that oppress marginalized groups. It does not seek to center communities or identities that are marginalized by including their experiences of racism and violence as part of their Catholic identities. The FOCUS missionary approach utterly neglects to engage in conversations about structural violence, poverty, racism, or sexism. Furthermore, this narrative does not account for the ways that Christianity has been or continues to be complicit in structural and cultural violence. Never in FOCUS materials is there an acknowledgement of the institutional sins of colonization, slavery, sexism, racism, and homophobia in the Roman Catholic Church. Rather, the deep story offered by FOCUS tells students that they are victims of a harmful culture.[13]

Yet, many students encounter and are impacted by institutional sins. Campus ministry should not ignore the experiences of these students. Instead, campus ministry should be a place in which students are safe to engage painful experiences and make meaning from them within their faith tradition. The narrative of the secular culture as something negative to be avoided encourages a sense of flight, a leaving of this culture (as if it is a bounded position or location) and fleeing to the safety of the Catholic Church. However, people's lived experiences are more complicated than this suggests. In fact, it is unwise and impossible to divorce a human person from the creative expressions, customs, and achievements of the various groups of people with whom they identify. Every person's experience is shaped by multiple structures and narratives that marginalize and oppress, as well as offer possibilities for privilege, safety, and hope.

LISTENING FOR NEW NARRATIVES

One way to counteract oppression created by a single narrative of what it means to be Catholic is to seek additional narratives. Each student's experience of God and living out their faith offers a treasure trove of material for broadening Catholic identity. Campus ministers seeking to respond pastorally to the needs of all their students may appreciate

---

practical questions to assist their efforts in creating a more welcoming and just campus ministry environment. Toward this end, students and missionaries may be invited to consider how their own life circumstances inform their faith:

- How would I describe my relationship with God? What stories might I tell that describe how my relationship with God developed?
- How do my life experiences as a human person (including race, culture, gender, socio-economic background, family background) impact my understanding of God? Or my sense of the sacred in my life?

In working with students, I would aim to draw them ever deeper into the lived, embodied, material experiences of themselves and those around them. Likewise, missionaries may be encouraged to consider the following as they listen to others' experiences even as they share their own.

Beyond the Narrative of Alienation

FOCUS offers testimonials of students on its website that serve as examples of the efficacy of FOCUS on college campuses. These testimonials further the narratives of conversion and discipleship FOCUS promotes. For example, Eliza Kelly, a FOCUS minister at Harvard, writes on her missionary page, "On college campuses plagued by loneliness, depression, substance abuse, and purposelessness, students are thirsting to know the Truth of the Gospel—that they are loved beyond comprehension and made for so much more than this world."[14] Eliza begins in the place that I think is the most important to begin: the context of the person to whom she desires to minister. I agree that theology begins in coming to understand one's own particular situatedness and the particulars of context and experience. Eliza here is pointing to the context she sees as the place for enacting theology, offering an example of James Cone's claim that "one's social and historical context decides not only the questions we address to God but also the mode or form of the answers given to the questions."[15]

I would invite Eliza into examining the troubling aspects of life on campus for the students that she encounters, identifying the particularities of each student:

- What in their past and present experiences has brought them to moments of desperation or alienation?
- How do they articulate what they desire?

As personal experience is fruitful ground for spiritual exploration, I would pay attention to how Eliza talks about her own experience and encourage her to explore times of desperation and alienation in her own life.

However, it is also important to consider Sylvia's response to experiences of alienation. What might Sylvia experience when she feels isolated by FOCUS's definitions of discipleship? What must it be like for Sylvia to be among a group of white peers who are resonating with the victimization motif FOCUS promulgates? What other experiences of alienation does Sylvia encounter in her daily life?

Alienation is an important reality for Eliza to explore because it takes different forms in people's lives. The move to universalize alienation might cause Eliza to miss important experiences of alienation in the lives of the students, particularly the lives of BIPOC and first-generation students. In exploring her own experiences of alienation, I would ask Eliza to be curious about the alienation others experience. I think that an orientation of wanting to learn about the alienation others experience would foster a continual process of helping Eliza see the "narrowness of [her] experience"[16] and the particularity from which she understands God. Questions that I would offer for her personal reflection include the following:

- What are you learning about the experiences of your students?
- How do these differ from your own?
- What more can you learn about their experiences?
- How does understanding someone else's experiences broaden your understanding of the world?
- What happens when you approach others' differences from a space of loving curiosity? Can you see how this might be different than fitting others' experiences into your framework of understanding?

I hope these questions would foster an orientation of drawing Eliza into her own particular struggles and pushing beyond them to wonder and learn about the truth of others' struggles.[17]

Beyond Turning from the Sinful Life

Another FOCUS missionary at Harvard, Stephen Hill, describes his undergraduate experience in this way:

> Immediately upon entering college, I went after the 'college dream' by living the party lifestyle; and in doing so I abandoned the Church. The longer and deeper I invested myself into this sinful life, the more I desired happiness, true friends, and love, which I was not finding in the way I was living. One day, after hitting rock bottom, I entered the university chapel and...came across a FOCUS missionary who eventually became one of my closest friends....If I had never met the FOCUS missionaries on campus, I would likely have never come back to the Church and would have been another fallen away Catholic, another soul consumed by the temporary pleasure of the world and not seeking anything truly meaningful.[18]

Stephen's narrative framing of meaning is cast in the theological terms "temporary pleasure of the world" versus "anything truly meaningful." This is another way of articulating a familiar dichotomizing of the "flesh" and the "spirit." He illustrates the aspect of FOCUS theology that sees things of "temporary pleasure of the world" or "the flesh" as bad and things of the Church and God, and "the spirit," as good. I find it challenging that this theology does not recognize that God dwells in the flesh of our lives. Additionally concerning, Stephen's identification of flesh as sinful risks further alienation of his own body. Equating the flesh with the sinful is to forget that humans, in their bodies, are made in the image and likeness of God and are declared to be "good" (Gen 1:26). I might invite Stephen to consider:

- "Flesh" is used here as a metaphor for sin. However, can you think of a positive experience of your body when you experienced it as a gift or a blessing?
- Are there potential consequences of viewing the body negatively?

It is also worthwhile for the campus minister and the missionary to consider Sylvia's experience alongside Stephen's. For Sylvia, participating in God's goodness is already embodied in her actions with her *abuelita* on behalf of her neighbors. Her joy in the gift of her God-given body is enfleshed through her dancing with others in her service organization. Might Stephen learn from Sylvia that the body and the spirit can be integrated in praise of God? Indeed, Jesus affirms the worthiness of human bodies through the incarnation, which may serve as a liberative understanding of God.

JESUS OFFERS A LIBERATIVE STORY

To root FOCUS missionaries in Scripture, I would draw their attention to Jesus' miracles. Jesus was very concerned about the bodily experience of people as he fed and healed them. Both his language and his actions in miracle stories speak of healing. In spending prayerful reflection with these stories, I would hope to help them come to see how the miracles of Jesus take the form of restoring physical and social health.[19] This emphasis of restoring social health speaks directly to the sense of alienation that the missionaries seek to heal among college students. I would emphasize how Jesus as the incarnation of the God of life demonstrates God's desire to heal the individual and restore communal relationships. Emphasizing the particularities of the missionary's experience, I would work to help them make connections regarding how their image of God arises from their experience. I would also draw them into exploration of God's covenantal relationship through a theme of liberation. For example, students and missionaries may be invited to consider:

- How do you image God? What characteristics does God have?
- When were you in need of healing?
- When did you experience healing? What was the source of that healing?
- Have you ever been a part of a group in need of healing? How did the group heal?
- How does your image of God impact your pathway to healing?

In addition to personal testimonial, FOCUS promotes evangelization through Bible studies. One of the Bible studies FOCUS gives to its missionaries to use with students focuses on God's covenants in the Old and New Testaments. "The Story of Salvation" Bible study ends with a session on Jesus as the fulfillment of God's covenant.[20] Fulfillment theology is potentially problematic because it promotes the oversimplification of Jesus as the fulfillment of the Old Testament. This approach places the Old Testament at the service of the New Testament. It encourages readers of the Bible to look for texts that serve as "proof" that Jesus is the fulfillment. Also, this approach implicitly invites either/or thinking where there is a clear "right" answer. New Testament vs. Old Testament, sacred vs. secular.

Rather than emphasize "Jesus as fulfillment" with the missionaries, I would raise questions about why "covenant" is meaningful in the texts and point to the themes of liberation. Here I would rely on liberation theologian Gustavo Gutierrez's understanding of covenant with the God of life. For Gutierrez, covenant is synonymous with liberation and justice: "Liberation, justice, and covenant imply one another; each is necessary for the full meaning of the others."[21] In this sense, covenant cannot be understood without liberation and justice. Without them, covenant does not achieve its full meaning. Additionally, God cannot be understood apart from liberation. As Gutierrez writes, "The God of life manifests love by forming a family of equals through an act of liberation in which God does, and demands, justice amid the people and enters into an irrevocable covenant with them in history."[22] In Gutierrez's understanding, the God of life, who is a God of love, demands justice.

The story of salvation as presented by FOCUS, does not engage the tools of biblical studies. The story is told as a linear narrative that can be known, codified, and memorized. It is delivered as a knowable message. No attention is given to any questions of historical-critical scholarship, hermeneutics, or readings from multiple perspectives. From a scholarly perspective, this drives me crazy. It is not good scholarship. But biblical scholarship is not the place to engage. However, instead of debating the finer points of biblical interpretation with FOCUS missionaries, it may be more fruitful to look for openings to discuss relationship:

- Who are the people in your life you are deeply committed to?
- What experiences cement your relationship with these people?

- How do you expect them to treat you? What expectations might they have of you? How are these expectations like a covenant?
- How do these relationships foster a sense of strength and freedom within you? What are you able to do because of these relationships?

I would further invite the missionaries see that their desire to overcome alienation is a desire for liberation. God desires that liberation for them and for all. Their desire for community is a reflection of loving what God loves—the healing, restoration, and liberation of the human family. The invitation to love what God loves asks more from disciples than Eucharistic adoration and telling people about Jesus. Gutierrez's insights regarding "the practice of justice" as an "intrinsic element of our relationship with God" may assist all would-be disciples in living their faith more fully.[23] Loving God in a covenantal relationship means that each person must explore the particulars of their life to see how they might be "practicing injustice" and work to dismantle or root it out of their life. Gutierrez also helpfully explains that worship is inseparable from the practice of ending injustice.[24] Thus, disciples' relationship with God will find greater fulfillment when they live and work for justice for all who are alienated.

CONCLUSION

What are the assemblages of those with whom we minister? As campus ministers, we seek to see our students and colleagues as whole people: as people situated in diverse experiences of trauma and grief, possibility and privilege, hope and desire. The variety of ways of living out their Catholicism are shaped by family and cultural histories, by narratives of success and progress, and by structures that racialize, oppress, or liberate.

Campus ministers are uniquely placed to help the FOCUS missionaries and students explore definitions of culture and society, stretching them to consider aspects of theology and identity currently neglected by the FOCUS missionary model. FOCUS also ignores how both its vision and the individual are constituted by all the components of the human experience. Instead, FOCUS theology promotes a white, middle-class narrative as a universalized norm for living Catholicism faithfully, which is highly problematic, especially for those who do not fit within that narrow definition of Catholicism.

Yet, FOCUS encourages missionaries to form "authentic friendships" with the people they serve: "In forming missionary disciples, it is not enough to pass on the Gospel message and the teachings of the Church. That is essential, but we must do more. We must genuinely love the people we are serving, accompanying them in life and personally investing ourselves in them through authentic friendship."[25] This aspect of FOCUS's evangelization method might serve as a starting point for engaging in a broader ministry.

This concept of authentic friendship functions as an entry point for examining intersectionality and particularity of people's experiences. Thus, missionaries may learn to move beyond a universalizing approach to theologizing. Instead of seeking ways that the individual fits into models or structures, they may discover how to honor the individual makeup of the person. By attending to their own situatedness, missionaries will reflect upon their own experiences:

- What stirs and empowers them?
- What nurtures their relationships with God?
- What traps them—trauma, grief, pain, loss, death, racism?
- Finally, what frees them to engage the wider community and participate in enacting justice in the world?

NOTES

1. Almost 800 FOCUS missionaries serve in 205 locations, primarily on college campuses across the United States. See "FOCUS Sends 800 Missionaries to 205 Locations to Share Evangelical Passion," FOCUS, July 15, 2021, https://www.focus.org/about/news-press-room/recent-press-releases/focus-sends-800-missionaries-to-205-locations-to-share-evangelistic-passion.

2. For deeper insight into the lived experiences of FOCUS missionaries, see Katherine Dugan, *Millennial Missionaries: How a Group of Young Catholics Is Trying to Make Catholicism Cool* (Oxford University Press, 2019).

3. FOCUS professes that "the Fellowship of Catholic University Students is a Catholic collegiate outreach whose mission is to share the

hope and joy of the gospel with college and university students, inspiring and equipping them for a lifetime of Christ-centered evangelization, discipleship and friendships in which they lead others to do the same." "What We Do," FOCUS, accessed November 18, 2021, https://www.focus.org/.

4. I do not intend to suggest that all BIPOC students struggle financially. Nor do I suggest that white students lack financial difficulty. Instead, I desire to create space within campus ministry for a range of experiences, with special attention to those who struggle the most— those who have to negotiate racial discrimination, as well as the difficulties of lower-income families.

5. Accessed January 20, 2021, https://www.focus.org/. The FOCUS website is updated regularly. Testimonials and general descriptions of the work of the organization may change over time.

6. For an example of internal diversity, see Lauren R. Kerby and Mary Perez, "Amy Coney Barrett and the Internal Diversity of American Women," Religious Literacy and Education, accessed November 18, 2021, https://religiousliteracyed.hds.harvard.edu/2020/10/23/amy-coney-barrett-and-the-internal-diversity-of-american-catholic-women/.

7. "Introduction: Transformative Discipleship," FOCUS, accessed November 18, 2021, https://focusoncampus.org/content/introduction-transformative-discipleship.

8. Dugan, *Millennial Missionaries*, 171.

9. Dugan, *Millennial Missionaries*, 4–5.

10. This approach to evangelization FOCUS dubs "The Main Thing" that they set out to achieve. "The Main Thing," FOCUS, accessed November 18, 2021, https://www.focus.org/about/the-main-thing.

11. "Introduction: Transformative Discipleship," FOCUS.

12. "Introduction: Transformative Discipleship," FOCUS.

13. For more on deep story and narratives of victimization within contemporary Christianity, see Lauren R. Kerby, *Saving History: How White Evangelicals Tour the Nation's Capital and Redeem a Christian America (Where Religion Lives)* (University of North Carolina Press, 2020). Further work could explore the resonances in the narratives on culture between FOCUS and white evangelical Christianity.

14. Benjamin and Eliza Kelly, "Where We Serve," accessed November 18, 2021, https://www.focus.org/missionaries/benjamin-eliza-kelly.

15. James H. Cone, *God of the Oppressed* (Maryknoll, NY: Orbis, 1997) 14.

16. Cone, *God of the Oppressed*, 14.

17. Cone, *God of the Oppressed*, xxii.

18. Stephen Hill, "My Story," accessed November 18, 2021, https://www.focus.org/missionaries/stephen-hill.

19. Gustavo Gutiérrez, *The God of Life*, trans. Matthew J. O'Connell (Maryknoll, NY: Orbis, 2013), 14.

20. "The Story of Salvation," FOCUS, accessed November 18, 2021, https://focusoncampus.org/content/the-story-of-salvation.

21. Gutiérrez, *The God of Life*, 2.

22. Gutiérrez, *The God of Life*, 2.

23. Gutiérrez, *The God of Life*, 16.

24. Gutiérrez, *The God of Life*, 47.

25. "A Vision for Missionary Discipleship: Win-Build-Send," FOCUS, accessed November 18, 2021, https://focusequip.org/a-vision -for-missionary-discipleship-win-build-send/.

Chapter 5

AROUND THE TABLE OF THE SACRED AND THE SECULAR

The Dinner Party

Lisa Cathelyn

As with many good finds, this one began with a haphazard Google search. Late one December night, I was hunched over my desk at the end of my first semester of theology studies. Google managed to interpret a combination of phrases, *young adult + grief + community + support*, and I stumbled upon The Dinner Party. The Dinner Party spans the globe and is a community of twenty- and thirty-somethings who have experienced the loss of a parent, friend, partner, child, or sibling. The Dinner Party's mission is to take one of the most isolating experiences, significant loss, and to create community through "the age-old practice of breaking bread."[1] Fueled by the adrenaline of the semester's end and the sheer disbelief at this organization's existence, I quickly submitted a digital application to be connected to a table. A few months later, I went to a stranger-turned-friend's Berkeley apartment and marveled at the mix of dark humor, honesty, and delicious food. I had found my people.

Let me rewind a bit. On August 17, 2011, the eve of my junior year of college, I nervously awaited the return of my parents to my childhood home in rural Illinois. They arrived in a daze after a day of tests and hard conversations at the University of Iowa Hospitals. My sixty-year-old father received a terminal diagnosis of metastatic prostate cancer with approximately twelve to eighteen months to live. Since I was physically away at school through most of my father's treatment, I was neither the primary caregiver nor a constant presence as rounds of chemotherapy, radiation, immunotherapy, and other incomprehensible medical terms unfolded during the fall and winter. That responsibility remained my mom's, his spouse for more than thirty years.

That fall, the weightiness and fog of grief, as well as the process of telling my inner circle of friends about my dad's diagnosis, hung over the academics and transition from a semester studying abroad. Lots of people talk about the difficulty of grief in the wake of a beloved's death. Few people openly commiserate about the grief that comes in the weeks and months *before* death, particularly in the context of terminal illness. Those pre-death waves of grief crash onto life's shore in a number of ways. I call those shocks to the systems that bring grief front and center the Grief Gut Check. These waves crash down when one observes the physical and/or psychological deterioration of a loved one, confronts questions of mortality in the shadow of terminal illness, or encounters grief's extraordinary heaviness in the midst of the mundane details of daily living. The Grief Gut Check floods in when I realize there will be certain milestones on the horizon where my dad's absence will be particularly felt, such as graduations or moves across the country. In retrospect, I notice that the weight of grief requires the creation of a different kind of space to hold these experiences.

As the year progressed, so did the cancer. A little more than ten months after diagnosis day, my father died on June 29, 2012, at home with our family surrounding him in our living room. In many ways, it was a good death: his wishes were honored, he had access to some of the best health care in the country, and there was time (though never enough) to settle financial and logistical matters. We were able to say heartfelt and teary goodbyes. Despite these graces, it still felt like a gut punch.

Where would I find support for this significant loss? Who would understand a young person's grief? There were bereavement support groups at the local parish available to my mom, who eventually became a leader of one of those groups. While my family had the common experience of grieving the same person, it remained a devastatingly lonely experience to live with the weight of grief. How could I navigate being a fatherless daughter? What is my response to the unintentionally invasive questions of where my parents—plural—live and work? At an unspoken level, I knew I couldn't be the only one avoiding awkward small talk about families or particular dates on the calendar.

The death of my father marked the second funeral in ten weeks for my family. Scarcely two months prior, my beloved auntie, my dad's only sibling, died in a hospital at the age of sixty-three. She also had cancer. My Auntie Sharon was one of the most loving, delightful people I was privileged to know. Our family was blessed by her creativity, her passion for education, and her constant presence at every recital, sporting event, and concert. I don't think she ever missed one. She demonstrated an unwavering support and love for others, and she was one of those people who made you feel so darn special. Perhaps the most heart-wrenchingly painful aspect of these two deaths was that I witnessed my paternal grandparents bury both of their children. As I prepared Auntie Sharon's eulogy, I recalled that she consistently entered any room and genuinely asked, "How are we doing?" In the months and years since I last heard Auntie Sharon utter those words, her question persists: How are we doing amidst the heaviness? Who can we turn to in our aching grief?

I will never forget the deep sense of peace and consolation in the week or so after my dad's death. It was truly a time when the faith of others carried me. The Facebook messages from high school acquaintances, the caravan of college friends who came from Wisconsin, and all the parishioners who wrote cards and paid their respects all made up a cloud of witnesses for us. This wider community of believers—whether professed aloud or not—created space for our family to walk through this unimaginable reality and its very real aftermath. Whether it was eating custard alongside friends in the basement; finding the house filled with breakfast casseroles, paper goods, and laughter; greeting extended family members who came in from across the country; or the quiet morning moments of peace, I felt deeply held by the prayers of others and by the physical accompaniment in those early days. I experienced a sense of warmth and consolation that I will never forget. As the months and years have passed, I wonder how to extend that sense of being held in prayer beyond the foggy, seemingly eternal, first days of life after loss. Grief is not linear, and even members of the same family unit experience the death of a loved one differently. So how do I continue to cope with the ongoing waves of grief?

Years later, on the heels of a stressful move and after the dreaded five-year death anniversary, I hopped into Sami's MINI Cooper. Sami was a new friend, and our kinship formed over our shared losses of parents. We wound through traffic to arrive in Stinson Beach, California. Within moments of our arrival, I felt a physical sensation of relief, the permission to breathe in the salty ocean air. It was so good to be surrounded by other young people who "get it," who have faced down dark days and possess the grit to tell the tale. We had arrived at the West Coast Dinner Party Host Retreat. We spent time in collective reflection and shared tips for hosting a group of strangers in our homes.

Oh, and the food! The delightful spread of magical charcuterie boards and delicious summer salads only served to enhance the space that allowed us to simply *be* with one another. There were no cell phone screens lingering beside our plates—in case of emergency, in need of a distraction—as we spent one evening gathered around multiple tables, dining alfresco.

When I first found The Dinner Party, I was astounded by just how many people were involved. Since its inception in 2010, in Los Angeles, The Dinner Party (TDP) has grown to over 400 in-person and virtual tables and has reached more than 10,000 Dinner Partiers. Prospective Dinner Partiers fill out an application, which is then reviewed by a community manager who hand-matches each individual to a particular table. There are affinity tables for specific types of loss or for those who hold particular identities, such as people who lost loved ones due to suicide or individuals who are Black, Indigenous, or People of Color (BIPOC). In the pandemic, a collective time that brought experiences of grief and loss to the forefront, TDP has shifted their methods and encouraged tables to gather over Zoom. They have also added one-on-one outreach through a "buddy system," where two strangers are matched to accompany one another in a virtual space. While the tables may be connecting as squares on a screen, the primary element remains: grief and loss for twenty- and thirty-somethings does not have to be an isolating experience. From the outset, hosts and Dinner Partiers recognize that no one is an expert in grief and that the loss of a beloved is not something one "gets over," but instead learns to carry forward with them in their lives. Hosts are not stand-ins for trained and capable psychotherapists; rather, they model candid conversations and peer support. During my initial introduction to this group, in the throes of my theological coursework, I could not help but draw deep parallels between the blessing, breaking, and sharing of the Eucharist in the chapel with the breaking of bread with my newfound friends in TDP.

Each time I connect with The Dinner Party, I find myself feeling a little less alone. Even though I know intellectually that *every person* on this planet will experience loss, it does not mitigate the feeling I have when someone—a stranger, a classmate, a friend—asks about my family. Will I be known as the fatherless daughter? Am I the friend who others will turn to when their person dies? The reality of losses throughout the world and the sheer scale of grief gives me pause. Every single day people are carrying around broken hearts and devastation. It certainly calls me to walk a little more gently on this planet and with a deeper reverence for people's resilience.

A year into being a Dinner Partier, I became one of the peer cohosts. Another ragtag group of survivors of loss—they should make badges for this—gathered in an East Bay home, a week or two before the holidays. I did not anticipate how powerful it would be to hold space for peers in grief. Squeezing around a table felt like a *kairos* experience, a mirror of liturgy where the lost and broken gather to break bread. For some of the young people present, this was the first Christmas/Hanukah/wintertime holiday without their beloved. Yet, there was a sense of abundance throughout the evening, with plenty of wine and yummy food. We gathered around a common table and shared silly and sad memories, as well as humble advice on how to take care of oneself in the onslaught of social media holiday posts. I remember feeling the "rightness" of cohosting, of holding space for others. I marveled at the everyday courage others demonstrated and the limits of certainty in life after loss.

Transitions and moves—particularly cross-country ones—bring out all the hard truths of grief. When I moved back to the Midwest, there were moments when I burst into tears over simple realities that I have now lived with for seven years. My dad will never lug boxes upstairs in my new home; I will not call my aunt and tell her about the higher educational institution where I now work. I will still root for the Cubs, my dad's beloved team, and I will still fumble, mentioning a dead parent on a date. I awkwardly dance around conversations with new coworkers who have banal questions such as, "So, where does your family live?" (*Do you mean my living or dead family members?*) I return to the city that held me in the early months of grief and to friends who knew me in the fog of it all.

A few months into my move, I have enough space—mentally and physically—to reconnect with The Dinner Party. The first time our table gathered in Milwaukee, it was December. Welcoming strangers into my apartment felt strangely normal since each person chooses to show up and speak their truths. The first dinner we had felt like an exhalation, a huge sigh of relief. As we went around introducing ourselves and the people who brought us to the table, I marveled at the unfiltered way people shared. No one checked their social media accounts; people listened intently. We all laughed and cried, as no glass remained unfilled.

Whenever Dinner Partiers gather, there are community guidelines that structure the space. We recognize that "I" statements are important and that there is no hierarchy of suffering in grief. One person's story of loss is not more or less painful than another's. We hold one another's experiences in confidence and nonjudgment, acknowledging that sometimes participation looks like silence and other times it is laughing at a funny memory. After those first few dinners in the gray of a Midwest winter, we check in on each other: *How's that new job going? What did you do to survive the holidays? Why are bereavement groups always held in terribly lit, sterile basements? How did you mark the anniversary of her death?* From my perspective, The Dinner Party is successful because it dares to exist in a space of both/and. It is *both* wonderful to love other humans, *and* we have no idea how to keep going when those humans are gone. We recognize that we need each other to navigate this new normal. One time when we gathered for brunch, we brought out sticky notes and wrote down all the inconsiderate, strange, and unhelpful comments people have actually told us. We read them aloud and shook our heads in frustration, aware that words ultimately fail in these fragile moments. I consider my pastoral role on a college campus. When a student experiences a loss, even though a response is part of my job and even though loss was a part of my college experience, I still wrestle with what to write. What words can make the devastation more bearable?

We pass delicious salads and fill up our wine glasses, knowing that grief requires space for unanswered questions. No matter how much we narrate our experiences with caregiving, or eulogizing, or being upset at our dead person, we will never have all the answers. It is a frustrating and liberating experience to hold this mystery.

In this most secular of spaces, I realize that this is the beauty of church at its best: a ragtag group of believers who share a common experience. Just as those who participate in The Dinner Party honor those who have gone before us and name the persons who bring us to the table, early Christian communities gathered in house churches to break bread together at the table as they remembered Jesus. These house churches held the memory of Jesus' life, death, and resurrection, and allowed a community of disciples to share their collective experiences.

Jesus not only releases us from the power of death through his resurrection but Jesus' relationships with his beloved friends illustrate for all of us how we are called to acknowledge and carry the weight and grace of loss. The Christian worldview asserts that even in the heartache and wailing, death does not have the final word. Throughout all the Gospels, we hear many stories of Jesus showing up to grieve, encountering someone who is dead, or being called upon to heal. People in Capernaum climb on roofs and lower their paralyzed friend into a home (Matt 9:1–8; Mark 2:1–12; Luke 5:17–24). Jairus's daughter is commanded to rise (Mark 5:22–42; Luke 8:41–56). Mary and Martha, Lazarus's sisters, grieve their brother's death and pointedly tell Jesus that if he had just been there, their brother would not have died (John 11:21). This poignant scene displays the universality of grief and loss:

> When Jesus saw her weeping, and the Jews who came with her also weeping, he was greatly disturbed in spirit and deeply moved. And he said, "Where have you laid him?"
> They said to him, "Lord, come and see." Jesus wept. (John 11:33–35)

Those gathered express their grief in heaving sobs and wailing, and Jesus is not a stoic, unaffected bystander. Rather, he asks where Lazarus has been laid to rest. In response to this exhortation to "come and see," Jesus moves from the home of beloved disciples into the more vulnerable space of the tomb. Jesus' proximity to grief and loss demonstrates that these are spaces ripe for discipleship. Elizabeth Schlusser Fiorenza writes of equality among the disciples in John's Gospel, which is embodied through their service to and love for one another.[2] Those who grieve are all equals in their experience of loss. Even Jesus grieved.

Similarly, the unofficial "family" members of The Dinner Party share in that mix of death and life. Dinner Partiers dare to encounter others' experiences and bear witness to the weeping on the grief journey. Our names may not be Martha or Mary, but we are on the journey in the village of Bethany together. In the years I have gathered with other Dinner Partiers around the table, the participants I have encountered claim various faith traditions, including Jewish, atheist, Hindu, Christian, and agnostic. Even as those who sit around the table may profess different beliefs—or none at all—the table remains a locus of radical welcome where the common denominator is grief. We have all been on separate paths that are eerily familiar. In a most humble way, The Dinner Party offers a model outside of church from which the pilgrim people of God can live out their discipleship as they process their grief.

Living into the tension of a secular understanding of a both/and paradigm, as The Dinner Party epitomizes, Christian communities are called to the already-not-yet reign of God here on earth. In an era where one in four adults in the United States reports feelings of isolation, faith communities must announce an alternative model of connection. Are our local churches equipped to do this prophetic work? As I cull lessons from The Dinner Party and explore how they might apply to churches, I only comment on my own particular experience of parish life. While there must be emphasis on Sunday liturgy and cultivating a worshipping community, I also wonder how table fellowship extends beyond the transubstantiation prayer and spills over into a more embodied practice of Eucharist, outside of Sundays.

There are certain limitations in drawing inspiration for a religious organization from a secular one. Yet, unpacking the possible gifts a secular organization offers our ecclesial communities is worthwhile. The Dinner Party has no creed, per se, but it recognizes the effects of shared, communal truths: "Life after loss is different than life before, grief isn't linear, and moving forward is not the same as moving on."[3] I wonder how this nuanced understanding of grief and life after loss might inform the pastoral care churches offer to the bereaved. Do churches emphasize that grief is not linear in their programming? How do churches address the particular needs of young people in loss? Are we hearing about the hard truths of the grief journey in homilies? Do our churches offer bereavement support at all? Of course, The Dinner Party does not use or promote the sacraments, a cornerstone in the Catholic faith. Yet, it is worth considering what we might glean from The Dinner Party's example of incorporating human connection outside a sacrament and extending it to the wider church community. Based on my lived experience, most young people do not seek formal bereavement support from a religious institution because grief support that caters to young people rarely exists within a church, synagogue, or mosque.

My experience in training as a host with The Dinner Party through webinars, phone conversations, and retreats demonstrates that digital and real-life connections are key to a thriving organization. Do parishes have the technical infrastructure to provide consistent communication and training to its members? I consider the "onboarding" process with the Dinner Party. It is a one-to-one relationship with a regional community manager and includes a training manual, follow-up calls, and regular check-ins. Beyond becoming a "registered" parishioner, do we "onboard" our members so that they feel more oriented to the community? What about those who are not registered? My sense is that most millennial Catholics, particularly those without young children, are likely not registered at their local parish. Anecdotally, I have friends who parish-hop and others who have not found a vibrant community outside of a college setting. How might an informal introduction, such as a potluck dinner, foster bonds in a local parish outside of Sunday Mass?

As a millennial who is neither a "none" nor a nun, I inhabit a space that can feel isolating: I am a Catholic feminist theologian. I wonder how to be a disciple of Jesus Christ and how God's call unfolds through my own grief journey. Beyond the perennial question of financial concerns—my call exists within the realities of basic needs such as food, health insurance, and a stable income—I also wonder how to counter the loneliness I experience in my professional work. I yearn for the ancient, sacred act of breaking bread together, to be commissioned and sent out like the first Apostles, surrounded and supported by other believers living their call to discipleship. My current context in in the Midwest allows me to reconnect with old friends while also serving as a campus minister at a women's college. Still, I wonder if I am the only politically progressive, in-my-bones Catholic out there. Surely, there are others. I am fortunate to connect with other women with whom I studied theology; we continue to support each other via text messages, calls, and emails. A group of us participate in regular *lectio divina* via video conference. As much as I appreciate digital spaces to connect, they are a supplement to, and not a replacement for, dependable, in-person connections. I stumbled upon a local parish during my first few months in the Midwest. It is a church that is small, welcoming, and gospel centered. This parish reflects the diversity of the city, announcing the reign of God in its own humble, honest way. They offer an evening Mass geared especially for young people and families. It feels like home; I feel less alone. I am not the only millennial who experiences isolation in their faith convictions.

Through my studies of theology and experiences of the Church at its best, I am led to ponder the connection between my own personal experience of grief and collective experiences of grief in the world. I consider the persistent presence of the women at the foot of the cross, bearing witness to Jesus' empire-sanctioned execution. Throughout all four Gospels, we hear that they were the ones who remained, even as others shouted, "Crucify him!" and looked on at the gruesome spectacle. The Gospels provide very little biographical information for these women at the foot of the cross. We know some of their names: Joanna, Salome, Mary of Nazareth, Mary the mother of James, and Mary Magdalene (Mark 15:40; Matt 27:55–56; Luke 23:49; John 19:25). How are we, the collective body of believers, consistently showing up and denouncing a culture of death? Amidst the violence, sorrow, and grief, we wrestle with the question of suffering. Bringing these questions to God is natural and essential for believers. However, we must also not lose sight of the call to be disciples in times of tragedy, mass shootings, and rampant ecological destruction. There is so much death around us. The example of the women gathered at the foot of the cross challenges us to show up in solidarity at the foot of the cross of today's crucified peoples. Like Joseph of Arimathea, we can carry the nard and help prepare a body for burial (Matt 27: 57–60; Mark 15:43–46; Luke 23: 50–53; John 19:38–40).

As we deal with the death that surrounds us, we must also check in on friends experiencing particular loss long after the initial waves of sympathy cards recede in the months after a burial or memorial service. The Dinner Party offers wisdom about how to proceed as disciples, as it recognizes there is no linear timeline in the aftermath of loss; whether it has been a year, two months, or seventeen years since a loved one has died, people reckon with this new normal in various ways. Sharing a meal, a cup of coffee, and being available to hear how someone is truly doing is a modern-day manifestation of carrying the nard in the dark.

The Gospel of John offers a portrait of discipleship in Mary Magdalene's visit to the tomb of Jesus. Likely bewildered, foggy in mind, perhaps disbelieving that her beloved friend was publicly killed, Mary Magdalene goes to the tomb with the prepared oils and spices for the body of Jesus (Mark 16:1–2). What was it like to walk to the tomb? The laborious task of describing in detail to this stranger in the garden her friend's violent and untimely death mirrors the heaviness in disclosing that a loved one is dead. It never gets easier to disclose. Still, it matters. A key moment in this scene is that Mary Magdalene is seen, recognized, and understood by Jesus. When she is called by name, she recognizes again her Teacher: *Rabbouni* (John 20:16). The risen Jesus tells her to carry the message to the other followers, who also are beset by grief and reckoning with a new normal. Mary Magdalene declares that she has seen the risen Lord, and everything has changed. Even if Mary Magdalene was initially dismissed by the other followers, the resurrection proclamation is powerful precisely because it unfolds *among* a community of believers. In hearing this news, perhaps the disciples felt a little less alone in their bewilderment.

I have learned that the boundaries between the sacred and secular are, in fact, blurry. The Gospel narratives are filled with grief in abundance, yet churches struggle to grapple with it. Grief is everywhere and touches every life. We have to deal with it, but churches fall short in offering support. Therefore, I needed to turn to secular spaces, like The Dinner Party, in order to find what I needed. I learned that sometimes secular spaces teach us how to be church.

Throughout my five years as a Dinner Partier, I have experienced a glimmer of what the early Christian communities cultivated in their house churches. Strangers-turned-friends gathered around a table as we attempt to make sense of the harrowing path of life, loss, and resurrection. As I examined the structure and core values of a secular organization, I find that it is precisely in this secular space where I have encountered the Divine and a deepening of my own ministerial call: a call to gather God's people together and simply be, to enter more deeply into relationship and to know that we are tasting a morsel of God's kingdom on earth. While there are certainly limitations to applying the wisdom of a secular organization as a model for the deeply sacramental life of the Catholic Church, I have learned that these spaces nourish my spirit and that of others, particularly those who are unaffiliated or have left an institutional church. This abundant, collective space operates in contrast to the sometimes-stifling hunger for connection I experience in the Catholic Church. In the years to come, as the global community grapples with tremendous collective trauma and grief due to the COVID-19 pandemic, may the body of believers proceed with a stance of humility, knowing there is much to glean from secular spaces such as The Dinner Party to encourage us to show up as disciples, bewildered and consumed by grief. We know that death does not have the final word, but that truth is easier to carry when held with others.

NOTES

1. The Dinner Party, accessed November 18, 2021, https://www.thedinnerparty.org/.

---

2. Elisabeth Schüssler Fiorenza, *In Memory of Her: A Feminist Theological Reconstruction of Christian Origins* (New York: Crossroad, 1983), 326.

3. "Dinner Partier Manifesto," The Dinner Party, accessed November 18, 2021, https://www.thedinnerparty.org/manifesto.

Chapter 6

BUILDING THE DOMESTIC CHURCH

Raising Children as a Progressive, Catholic Mamá

Kristina Ortega

I begin every morning as the dawn silently creeps through my bedroom window and the birds in the trees begin to chirp, slowly and blissfully awakening me to a new day. This momentary peace abruptly ends with, "Wake up! Get out of bed! Stop hitting your brother! Brush your teeth! We're going to be late!" In forty minutes flat, my children, my husband, and I have dressed, eaten the cereal bars that count as breakfast, prepared lunches, made beds, packed backpacks, poured coffee, and confirmed the afternoon plans about meetings, practices, and dinner before we are out the door.

Twice a week we also help our sons tie their neckties, a required part of the Mass uniform at their Catholic elementary school. Every day, I spend five minutes practicing mindfulness with my seven-year-old, who has decided on his own to set a mantra for each day. He adopts phrases like "I am kind to others; I am kind to myself" and "ready to learn, ready to love." As we walk down the narrow hallway in our house, we pass our tiny home altar residing in what was intended to be the built-in niche for a landline phone. My boys endlessly rearrange the collection of holy cards that sit on the little ledge next to the hand-carved figure of Mary I bought while leading an immersion trip to Guatemala, the icon of Christ Sophia given to me by the theology department at my university when I graduated, and a bottle of holy water from the Chalice Well in Glastonbury. As they tie their shoes, they sit on a couch under a framed poster from a conference I helped to coordinate while in grad school. The poster reads: "Know color, know God. No color, no God?" They eat their breakfast at the table under the watchful eye of a framed print of an angel, which they know we purchased at the annual auction supporting the urban, Catholic, all-boys high school where their father once taught. As they walk out the front door, they pass an assortment of small crosses, gifts, and souvenirs from past travels. A mezuzah I bought in the Old City Market in Jerusalem before either of them was born accompanies this collection. When the boys were little and they were afraid to sleep in their room, we used to tell them that by pushing on the three yellow tiles on the mezuzah we were activating the force field around our house that kept us safe. On our mantle, next to the Colorado Rockies bobbleheads and the Yasiel Puig "Puigy Bank," you will find a devotional candle adorned with the image of the Virgen de Guadalupe. The shelf in the boys' room includes books like *Dear Pope Francis* and *Telegrams to Heaven: The Childhood of Archbishop Oscar Arnulfo Romero* stacked among *Harry Potter*, *Percy Jackson*, and *Magic Tree House* books.

We go to Mass on Sunday (okay, most...okay, many Sundays), but we choose to pass half a dozen parishes on our way to Dolores Mission Parish, a small, poor, Jesuit, mostly Latino community nestled between rapidly gentrifying neighborhoods and low-income housing. For a brief time, I volunteered at Homeboy Industries, and my husband spent a year as a Jesuit Volunteer in Los Angeles. Both experiences brought us to Dolores Mission. Its mission and ethos are central to the spirituality of our family. Our kids take for granted that the female pastoral associate works side by side with the pastor. They do not realize it is an unusual privilege to hear her voice when she, on occasion, offers a reflection after communion. They assume that every church opens its doors at night to allow homeless men to sleep on cots in the sanctuary. They never ask why Mike, who lives at the Catholic Worker house, prays every Sunday for an end to the "imperial war machine and the capitalist system that undergirds it." To them, that is just what people in church do. In addition, doesn't every family spend time at their local

Jesuit Volunteer house, where young adults spend a year in service and simple living? As a family, we do things like Stations of the Cross on Good Friday and *Las Posadas* (enactment of Joseph and Mary seeking a room at an inn) at Christmas. There is nothing unique in these practices themselves. However, our *via crucis* and *caminatas* take us through the streets of Boyle Heights, once the gang capital of Los Angeles and a neighborhood many people avoid.

Our Catholicism is probably the most defining characteristic of our family. I suppose my husband and I, as millennials, are the exception to the trend of waning religious affiliation. Our peers tend to be "spiritual but not religious," if anything at all. Our reasons for *why* we stay are many and complicated, and not the focus of what I want to share. Instead, I would like to explore *how* we stay. Specifically, how do I, as a Catholic mom, create space in my home, in my life, and in the lives of my children to be church? How do I create a space where we are prophetic, sacramental, joyful, humble, hospitable, and healing? I would like to make clear at this point that I use the pronoun "I" because my focus is my motherhood and not because I am alone in my endeavor to create church. My marriage is a true partnership, and my husband stands with me in all I do. I could just as easily write "we," but I will let him speak for himself when he writes his own book!

Recognizing the wisdom of postmodernism, I feel obliged to locate and contextualize myself. I am a forty-year-old cradle Catholic. I am both a fourth generation Angeleno and the daughter of an immigrant. I prefer the cultural label Chicana. I am a straight, cisgendered, married woman. I hold two degrees in Catholic theology. I work full time as a teacher in a Catholic secondary school, and I am also a dancer trained in classical ballet and modern dance. These facets of my identity that I name are not arbitrary nor incidental. Each plays a very specific role in how I raise my children, how I practice my faith, and how I build church.

My own mother came of age at the height of the Second Vatican Council. She took its renewal and reforms to heart. Consequently, my religious upbringing was infused with the messages of the groundbreaking documents from this council. Because of this, I regularly turn to *Gaudium et Spes*, *Sacrosanctum Concilium*, and *Nostra Aetate*[1] for inspiration, clarity, and direction on all matters, including family life. The Dogmatic Constitution on the Church, *Lumen Gentium*, promulgated by Pope Paul VI in 1964, speaks of the role of the family in this way:

From the wedlock of Christians there comes the family, in which new citizens of human society are born, who by the grace of the Holy Spirit received in baptism are made children of God, thus perpetuating the people of God through the centuries. The family is, so to speak, the domestic church. In it parents should, by their word and example, be the first preachers of the faith to their children; they should encourage them in the vocation, which is proper to each of them, fostering with special care vocation to a sacred state.[2]

While I acknowledge that Pope Paul VI was certainly writing within a context that defines families in the most traditional and narrow way, I don't think we need to throw the baby out with the baptismal font water. There is a certain wisdom and beauty in the pope's words. I take very seriously my vocation as a Catholic mother to raise, form, and nurture responsible citizens and to build my own "domestic church." It is no easy task to create a functional domestic church in the midst of #NunsToo and the Pennsylvania Grand Jury Report. How do I navigate this if not with patience, courage, nuance, and joy? I am not talking about a naïve, simplistic joy that says, "Everything is okay," but the joy found in the gospel message. I am inspired by the joy of the Visitation, the joy Jesus felt when gathered with his friends, and the joy of a message of rebirth after tragedy. Pope Francis speaks of joy in *Evangelii Gaudium* when he says, "This is the joy which we experience daily, amid the little things of life....'My child, treat yourself well, according to your means....Do not deprive yourself of the day's enjoyment' (Sir 14:11, 14). What tender paternal [or maternal] love echoes in these words!"[3]

Fr. James Martin, SJ, writes in his book *Between Heaven and Mirth: Why Joy, Humor, and Laughter are at the Heart of the Spiritual Life,*

But if our lives on earth provide us with a taste of heaven, as I believe they do, then we may assume heaven includes laughing with friends and family....So be joyful. Use your sense of humor. And laugh with the God who smiles when seeing you, rejoices over your very existence, and takes delight in you, all the days of your life.[4]

My Catholicism is a faith that brings me deep and profound joy and consolation despite many moments of anger and frustration.

Hopefully, I am also embodying what Pope Paul VI encouraged parents to exemplify: living as an example and preacher. I witness my faith to my children by encouraging free thought, exposing them to different worldviews, and fostering critical conversation surrounding tough ideas. I think I am starting to see this witness to faith bear fruit. Not too long ago, my younger son said to me, "They say 'God the father,' but they should really say 'God the mother' because God made me, and I was made in your tummy. So, God is more like a mommy than a daddy." My first thought was, "Is he old enough to read *She Who Is*?"[5] Then I calmed down and reveled in the wonder of a five-year-old's first deeply theological thought and in the momentary sweetness of his not knowing the radical nature of that thought.

Pope Paul VI further instructs parents to foster each child's vocation. Right now, the boys' vocation seems to be blacksmithing. They have designed their forge and selected a logo and a business name (Viking Forge, if you're interested). I have overheard them discuss the option of marriage and fatherhood. They have both decided that they want to be uncles but not fathers. I am not sure how that is going to work out, but I will let them run with it for a while! My own parents gave me the freedom to study and pursue what made me happy. That freedom is precisely what led me to go to a Catholic university, study theology, and become a Catholic educator. I will give the same freedom to my sons. They may pursue whatever they want. I am not sure how I would feel if one of them receives a call to the priesthood. On one hand, who am I to stand in the way of an authentic vocation? On the other, how can I give my children over to a deeply flawed structure in need of reexamination and healing? However, if one of them chooses that path, then I am grateful to the pastors and associate pastors of Dolores Mission Church for modeling a priesthood marked by collegiality, listening, empathy, cultural competency, community-based decision-making, servant leadership, humility, and a life of simplicity.

My cultural background intertwines with my faith. My family has a complicated immigration story, but the simple version is that my grandfather brought his wife and two young children from Mexico to Los Angeles in 1949. Living in Los Angeles in the 1950s and 1960s, my father faced incredible prejudice from teachers, coaches, and neighbors. I have never spoken directly to him about the prejudice he experienced. However, I have observed that he has reacted to his childhood by raising his own children as "American." He taught us to speak only English so that we would be able to "pass" as they say. I sometimes consider it ironic that I am intentionally reclaiming and celebrating my heritage to the point of choosing not Hispanic, or even Latina, but Chicana as my preferred label. What does this have to do with making space and creating church? Everything! Chicana is the flavor of my Catholicism. It means that my sons have been able to tell you the story of *La Virgen* and Juan Diego since they could speak. It means that they know a funeral is not just one day but nine days of gathering with family and praying the rosary. It means that we take *compadrazgo*, the intense reciprocal relationship among parents, godparents, and godchildren, very seriously. There is also a political dimension to the word Chicana. This means that our faith and our culture impel us to attend marches in support of DACA and Dreamers, against family separation, against pipelines, and stand in solidarity with public school teachers as they strike for better wages and working conditions. The church I create in my home is a church of action. Because of their faith and their culture, my children will *be* better, *do* better, and, as Greg Boyle, SJ, says, "create a community of kinship such that God might recognize it."

Long before I was married or had children, I chose to pursue the precarious academic path of theology. In my sophomore year at Loyola Marymount University (LMU), I declared theology as my minor. At the end of my junior year, because of an injury, I made the decision to drop my dance major to a minor and finish my BA through the theology department. You know the joke about how Catholics do not read the Bible? Well, it was true, at least for this Catholic. It was not until I stepped into the classrooms of Dr. Jeff Siker and Dr. Judy Yates Siker, both ordained Presbyterian ministers, as well as Dr. Daniel Smith-Christopher, a Quaker, that I fully grasped the depth and richness of the Hebrew and Christian Scriptures. Through the gifted scholarship of Judy, Jeff, and Daniel, I was inducted into a world of Hebrew, Greek, and Aramaic etymology and wordplay, textual criticism, and sacred myth. I learned how to read a commentary, a Gospel parallel, and side-by-side translations. More importantly, I learned to read Scripture with joy. Other than their academic brilliance, my primary memory of each of them is the manner in which they embodied joy. I am certain that their excitement for teaching Scripture is exactly why I ended up doing what I am doing now. A few years later, when I started my master's studies at LMU, I was ready to deepen my own spirituality and theology. I began this program less than one year after 9/11. Perhaps, I was looking for answers, or simply consolation, in a time of global upheaval and ecclesial unrest. If my undergraduate studies were about discovering what a text said, my years in graduate school were about what went unsaid, as well as whose voice was left out. During this time, I learned words that would become my foundation—words like *Mujerista* (theology that centers on the experiences of Latinas), liberation, Womanist, and *comunidad de base* (grassroots community). I discovered authors of books that would become my personal canon: Ada Maria Isasi-Diaz, Delores Williams, Chung Hyun Kyung, and Elizabeth Johnson. I found very few answers but learned how to ask the right questions.

My motherhood, my Catholic motherhood, is profoundly shaped and influenced by my experience and studies in college and grad school. When the boys come home from school on the day of their weekly class Mass, I ask what the readings were and what they thought about them. I always start with "Oh, that's one of my favorites." They always reply, "You say that about all the readings. They can't all be your favorite." In the three or so minutes in the car that I have their attention before we move on to conversations about their favorite toy or who is the stronger superhero, we break open the readings and engage in a little lesson. In the car following a Mass that must have included a reading about God talking to Moses or Jesus delivering the Beatitudes, my older son said to me, "Mom, I know why your school is on a mountain. It's because God hangs out on mountains, so the nuns wanted to be closer to God." A first-grade exegesis and application at its finest! Around the same time, my genius son and I also had this exchange:

"Mom, did you know that some people think that girls can't do the same things as boys?"

"I did. What do you think about that?"

"I don't think that's okay." My son pauses and continues, "I've never seen a girl priest at church like Fr. Ted or Fr. Scott."

"You're right. Girls can't be priests. Did you also know that in some places girls aren't allowed to go to school or learn to read or have a job?"

"I'm going to write a letter to the president and Pope Francis and tell them that I don't think that's fair."

Children have an innate sense of right and wrong. (To test this theory give one child a slightly smaller piece of cake than the other and see what happens.) However, I would like to take a little credit for encouraging my kids to see what is not there, to see what is missing, and who is not at the table (or altar). As they grow into their privilege as white, urban, educated, American, Christian, men, I hope that my sons will be guided by the love and joy of Sacred Scripture that calls them to see the invisible and hear the voiceless.

Since 2001, I have taught theology in Catholic secondary schools. I have taught courses in Scripture, morality, social justice, church history, vocations, sacraments, and introduction to Catholicism in coed and all-girls settings. I have taught in the city and in the suburbs. I have taught the sons and daughters of incredible privilege and students on full scholarship. I have taught domestic day students and international boarding students, fourteen-year-old ninth graders through eighteen-year-old twelfth graders. I have taught well-catechized and churched Catholics, combative Catholics, traditionalist Catholics, Jews, Muslims, Buddhists, Hindus, Sikhs, agnostics, nontheists, and atheists. In my years as a novice teacher, I fell victim to the adage "Don't smile until Christmas." I walked into a classroom like Debbie Allen's character in FAME who boldly proclaimed, "Dance is the hardest department in the school." Well, I wanted to say, "Religion is the most important subject at our school." The way to prove its importance, I thought, was to make my students memorize all the details, take the hardest tests, and write the longest papers.

A little over ten years ago, I met and began to work with an incredible educator and activist who came to the school I was working at to lead workshops about diversity and inclusion. Calvin Terrell, a Phoenix-based speaker, facilitator, and community organizer, completely flipped my world as a teacher upside down. Through Calvin's influence, I have learned that each student who walks into my classroom deserves to feel like my favorite, deserves to be treated as an individual, and deserves to feel safe. Because of his workshops, I evolved from a content-based teacher to a relationship-based teacher. Although Calvin himself does not identify as Christian, through him I made what now seems like an obvious connection between my work and faith. I wanted to teach as Jesus did. If I was going to teach about Jesus, should I not also teach like Jesus? I imagine how the Samaritan woman at the well (John 4), or Zacchaeus (Luke 19:1–10), or the woman who was bent over (Luke 13:11–13) must have felt while in Jesus' presence—safe, seen, known, heard, loved, and freed. While my course content is important, I might be the only adult that students have in their lives who greets them with a smile, shows interest in their day, and cares about the kind of people they are becoming. I may be the only person who says, "I see you. I hear you. I love you." This is what makes students feel safe. Only when a classroom becomes a safe space can real learning happen.

This is also how I raise my own children and build our domestic church. My sons know that the correct answer to the question, "What is my number one job?" is, "To keep us safe." They currently believe this means keeping them from running into the street or burning themselves on the stove. What I hope they will one day appreciate is that it also means making them feel safe to take risks, try something new, fail, and try again. Allowing them to feel safe permits them to explore the full spectrum of emotions, not just the limited range traditionally allowed for men in our culture. I hope they feel that this is not a conditional safety. Our love and protection come with no strings; they are not based on grades, scores, or athletic achievements. The twentieth-century theologian Henri Nouwen tells us that who we are is more than what we do, what we have, or what others say about us.[6] We are the beloved sons and daughters of God, and on us God's favor rests. My love for my sons and the way I interact with them is based on their inherent human dignity and the *imago Dei* stamped on their souls. Each night, as I tuck them in bed, I say, "I love you, I am proud of you, and God made you perfect just the way you are." This is what I learned about parenting from being a teacher. This is what Jesus said to his followers. This is what a church should say to its members. After my nightly reminder, the boys have started to reply, "Right back at ya." My prayer for them is that they do not just return that message to me but spread it to everyone they encounter, building up the kingdom of God one person at a time.

When I was a senior in high school, I chose a line from a contemporary Irish hymn as my yearbook quote: "Dance, then, wherever you may be. I am the Lord of the dance said he!" Until that point, my dance life consisted of girls with one body type in pink tights and black leotards, end of the year recitals, and high school dance teams. I had no idea that I was about to step into a world of breath and release, falls and floor work, bodies of all shapes and sizes, and the most incredibly supportive community whose love and friendship continues to carry me even today. Perhaps all college dance departments are like this, or maybe the Department of Theater Arts and Dance at Loyola Marymount was special and unique. It was in its dance studios, stages, and dressing rooms that I learned not only to honor my own body—to listen to it when it was tired or injured—but also to see the beauty and the glory of God in every human's shape, size, ability, gender, or orientation. Dance is the space where body, mind, and soul meet. Dance is celebration and mourning, ethereal and grounded, transcendent, and immanent. Dance is prayer. Today, I continue this prayer when I serve as a minister of liturgical movement at various gatherings throughout the Archdiocese of Los Angeles. As a teacher, I am aware of and try to respond to all the different ways my students need to learn—visually, aurally, and kinesthetically. I believe that pastors and liturgists also have a responsibility to respond to the different ways people of faith need to connect with God. Some need silent contemplative prayer, some need the ritual of the Mass, and some need to sing in the choir. I need to dance, and, as I have been told, some need to see dance as a tangible manifestation of the movement of the Spirit.

In my home, my domestic church, all bodies are good, whole, and holy. We love. We pray and discuss spiritual matters. We study and are a family of readers. We also ride bikes, swim, hike, and host impromptu dance parties in the living room. Hearts, souls, minds, *and* bodies are nurtured and celebrated. We talk about being healthy rather than being skinny. We serve healthy food but also recognize that the occasional ice cream cone or a doughnut after Mass is not the worst thing in the world. Recently, my older son was musing on conscience and choice when he said, "The best gift God gave us was free will. The second best was taste buds." My sons know that both intellect and sensuality come from God. Mind is not above body. Mind and body (and heart and soul) deserve care. We treat our bodies with gentleness and the bodies of others with respect. We use our minds and bodies to discover and connect with God. Through our intellectual pursuits, as well as our physical actions, we share the good news so that others may receive it.

Being a mother today is not easy. Mothers are pushed and pulled by our family's needs, our own aspirations, and society's expectations. Being a Catholic today is also not easy. All too frequent headlines of financial and sexual scandal, limits based on gender and orientation, and a hierarchy seemingly out of touch with the people make it very easy to just walk away. I try to focus on all that is good in the Church and stay connected to the core of our beliefs. The banner picture of a Facebook group I follow sums up my goal as a Catholic mom: "As for me and my house, we will serve the Lord...and systematically decimate capitalism, racism, and cisheteropatriarchy." In my home, we are planting the seeds of what the Church can and must be.

When the day is done and the dishwasher has been loaded, showers taken, teeth brushed, one last fight mediated, tomorrow's work clothes ironed, and the lights turned off, before I drift off to sleep, I lay my head on my pillow and review my day. I ask *La Virgen* to protect my children as they sleep, consider the places I encountered God, look ahead to how I can be a better mother tomorrow, and whisper, "Thank you, God, for my children. Thank you, God, for my home. Thank you, God, for helping me to build tomorrow's church. Amen."

NOTES

1. Second Vatican Council, *Gaudium et Spes* (The Pastoral Constitution on the Church in the Modern World), December 7, 1965; *Sacrosanctum Concilium* (the Constitution on the Sacred Liturgy), December 4, 1963; and *Nostra Aetate* (Declaration on the Relation of the Church with Non-Christian Religions), October 28, 1965, https://www.vatican.va.

2. Paul VI, *Lumen Gentium*, The Dogmatic Constitution on the Church, November 21, 1964, Vatican website, https://www.vatican .va/archive/hist_councils/ii_vatican_council/documents/vat-ii_const _19641121_lumen-gentium_en.html, sec. 11.

3. Francis, *Evangelii Gaudium*, apostolic exhortation, 2013, accessed November 19, 2021, https://www.vatican.va/content/francesco/ en/apost_exhortations/documents/papa-francesco_esortazione-ap _20131124_evangelii-gaudium.html, sec. 4.

4. James Martin, SJ, *Between Heaven and Mirth: Why Joy, Humor, and Laughter Are at the Heart of the Spiritual Life* (San Francisco: Harper-One, 2012), 236.

5. Elizabeth A. Johnson, *She Who Is: The Mystery of God in Feminist Theological Discourse* (New York: The Crossroad Publishing Company, 1992/2002).

6. Henri Nouwen, "Being the Beloved," Sermon at the Crystal Cathedral, 1992.

Chapter 7

"HOW, THEN, AM I TO RESIST MY NATURE?"[1]

Liberation through Liturgy and Love

Elaina Jo Polovick LeGault

I have always loved liturgy and ritual. It was part of my childhood, my family, my faith, and every part of my life. In the morning when my mom drove my sisters and me to school, we recited prayers together. When there was a storm, my mother would take a dried palm she had saved from Palm Sunday, light it on fire, and carry it out onto our porch. The smoke would rise up to the sky while we prayed the Hail Mary and Memorare, asking Mary to wrap her mantle around our house. I soaked up the spiritual practices of my Polish Catholic family, as well as the liturgies and rituals of the Church. These rituals, and the women who taught them to me, led me to create my own prayer experiences as a teenager.

When I was eighteen years old, I prepared my first liturgy. My grandmother, whom we called "Gram," had lung cancer and was nearing the end of her life. When Dad was tasked with planning the funeral service for Gram, my parents asked me to help. I immediately sought out my high school campus minister in order to borrow the Order of Christian Funerals and as many prayer books as I could carry. I remember poring over the books and feeling the weight of my work. Drawing from the Catholic tradition, I crafted a liturgy for Gram. I reworded prayers, edited traditional rubrics, and put together an original liturgy I thought she would love. I was proud of my efforts, and I hoped they would bring my family peace when the time came. A few months later, Gram passed away.

Although I have no memory of the exact words of the liturgy or the precise scripture passages I had chosen, I remember distinctly the feeling of being at that liturgy. As my dad led us in liturgy and read the words I had written, I felt Jesus reaching out and touching my heart through those words. They were no longer mine. Instead, they were both a gift to my family and a gift tenderly given back to me. I felt a peace deep within myself, as well as a sense of courage and strength in realizing that God had worked through me. Looking around at my aunts, uncles, and cousins, I saw these words affect and console them, and I discovered the power of liturgy.

Writing my funeral service for Gram was an act of intimate love. The power of creating a liturgy, not just for her but for those she left behind, opened up a space for us to be transformed by our memory of her and the comfort of God's presence. I had no idea at the time, but looking back, it was the start of my unofficial vocation as a liturgist. This opportunity afforded me an incredible grace, to see the creative power of the Spirit at work in liturgy.

GOD CALLS

My love for liturgy and ritual has always been a part of me, and it has been a source of transformation throughout my life. One pivotal liturgy in my life was a diaconate ordination I attended when I was about twelve years old. When my childhood church received a new deacon, the whole parish was invited to attend the ordination at the basilica at the University of Notre Dame. People filled the basilica, and I remember the hum of excitement as we settled into our seats. When I saw the deacons lying prostrate on the ornate marble floor, I suddenly felt the presence of God in a way I had never experienced before. Something stirred deep inside of me. God was with me, and I had an overwhelming feeling that I was called to join those deacons on the floor. In that moment, I didn't consider how strange or illogical this feeling was. All I knew was that I wanted to lay down before God too—not just in that moment, but throughout my whole life. I had a mystical experience where I could see myself as a woman, wearing an *alb* and giving everything to Jesus as I myself laid my whole body down on that marble. I heard God calling me to be a priest.

At that time, I had never heard anyone talk about women's ordination, and I didn't even know that there were other Christian denominations with women priests. I knew that women could not be Catholic priests, but in my twelve-year-old mind that no longer made sense. For the first time I wondered, why can't women be priests? My encounter with the Divine and my vision of my own future had felt so real and clear that I couldn't believe there wasn't a place for this call in the only church I knew and loved. I remember that experience with great clarity. In the hours, days, and years since then my sense of call remains with me.

When I started to ask the adults around me why women couldn't be priests, I never received a satisfying answer. The adults in my life explained that Jesus was a man and so only men could be priests. This argument didn't really make sense to me since Jesus was also God, and it was quite obvious to me that priests were not God. Thus began the perpetual cycles of confusion and disappointment in a church that claimed to uphold the dignity and equality of women, yet would not take my vision seriously. I felt hurt that I could so easily be dismissed, and for the next fifteen years, I would fall in and out of love with the Catholic Church.

Throughout high school, I became increasingly involved in campus ministry as I led retreats and faith-sharing groups, and I continued to fall in love with liturgy. I was one of the few students who showed up at school an hour early to attend 7:00 a.m. Mass in my high school's small brick chapel. I felt at home in that dark and quiet place and visited when I had extra time during lunch. I talked to Jesus all the time and we became good friends. I talked to him about how much I despised my religion teachers who taught fervently about sin. I sat in the chapel thinking about Mrs. Jones telling us it was her job to make sure we didn't burn in hell, and I wondered why no one taught us about the love I felt from God. I experienced a disconnect between the presence of God I encountered in prayer and what I was taught in the classroom. Thankfully, even in the midst of this tension, the Spirit continued to draw me close. It is hard to put into words my experience of call at that time other than I felt God's love and also felt a call to give my life to the work of the Church. My mind would often drift back to that diaconate ordination, and I would wonder what it would be like to join those lying prostrate before God.

My heart longed to join these men of God. Yet, there was a profound separation between the God I was coming to know and my experience of the priests of my community who stood *in persona Christi*. I found myself disappointed with homilies, experiences in confession, and the conversations I had with my parish and school priests. Perhaps it was my familiarity with a priest who was a family friend, or maybe it was the way my other grandmother, Grandma Josephine, acted with her own self-proclaimed authority to bless us and give us dispensation from Mass whenever a priest would not, but I was not afraid of priests. On multiple occasions, I asked the priests to sit down and talk to me about things that were bothering me about the parish or school. My parents supported me and encouraged me to be an advocate for myself. Although I stood up to these men with conviction, I always left feeling belittled, chastised, or ignored. They talked about money and the inspiration people derived from expensive items in the Church while I was concerned about the just treatment of all people. I was taught in school to listen to these men without question and to respect them for their generosity and selflessness. Yet, as I listened to the priests and theology teachers speak about God's love and justice, I never saw or heard them practicing what they preached.

I had an epiphany about this when, as a senior in my high school, I was in a production of *The Crucible*, a dramatized and partially fictionalized story of the Salem witch trials, where the Puritan leaders begin to question and imprison everyone in town as hysteria takes over. I played the small role of Ezekiel Cheaver, the scribe who takes notes when the accused "witches" are put on trial. I can't remember a single line I said, but I clearly remember one line from John Proctor, a local farmer who has become disenchanted with the Church and skeptical of the witch trials. John Proctor addresses the local reverend who is questioning his church attendance and says, "A minister may pray to God without having golden candlesticks upon the altar…and when I look to heaven and see my money glaring at his elbows—it hurt my prayer, sir, it hurt my prayer."[2] John, who is a humble farmer, can't stand to see the new golden candlesticks that show the wealth and power of the Church when there are people in the community suffering. I too saw the golden candlesticks on the altar, and it hurt my prayer.

When I heard this as a high school student, it struck a deep chord with me. I saw so much injustice and so many people in need in the world and in my community. Yet, it seemed like my parish priest constantly preached about money. I saw not just golden candlesticks on the altar, but on the walls, statutes, and steeples, and it hurt my prayer. In John Proctor's words, I also heard Jesus saying, "Is it not written, 'My house shall be called a house of prayer for all the nations? But you have made it a den of robbers'" (Mark 11:17), as he cleansed the temple. In addition to the hypocrisy I saw, I had also recently told a trusted teacher about the call I felt to be a priest and was shocked when he told me there were other Christian denominations with women priests. My mind was blown. If women priests existed, why couldn't we have them? When I imagined Jesus flipping over tables and raging against the money changers, I wanted to join him. I wanted to flip over our Eucharistic table that only men are allowed to stand behind and say, "Jesus invites women to the table too!" I was angry at the patriarchy of the Catholic Church that oppressed and stifled me, and I felt rage that women couldn't be priests. I felt rage that I couldn't be a priest.

Despite this anger, the Catholic Church was all I knew, and I knew God was calling me to be a leader in the Church however I could. I started spending more and more time with the amazing campus minister at my school. She invited me to help plan Mass, Stations of the Cross, and retreats. She invited me to lead prayers and give talks on retreats. She empowered me, encouraged my gifts, and helped me write my first full liturgy for Gram. As I began to think about college and looking at majors, I remember walking into her office one day and asking her what education I needed in order to do what she did. She told me that she had majored in theology, did a year of service, and then gotten a master of divinity. It sounded like a good plan to me, and I eventually followed this path.

As I spent more time in the chapel and in the ministry office, the nuns that worked at my school quickly took notice and invited me to the vocation group. Between the fondness for the compassionate and fun nuns I met growing up and the fact that I was not allowed in the boy's vocation group, I decided to join. I grew to love the nuns who taught me about Clare of Assisi and her friendship with Francis, as well as the way their habits made their smiles seem even more joyful. I remember sitting in multiple chapels across the Midwest asking Jesus, "Do you want me to be a nun?" He never responded, which I took as a "no." I loved being with the nuns, but never felt like I wanted to be one of them. Still, these nuns and my campus minster were the ones who introduced me to spiritual direction and true discernment. Being a part of the vocation group also deepened my relationship with my great-aunt Sister Paschalita. When Sister Paschalita visited, it was like an extra light was turned on in the room. She had a glow of love and joy that she shared with my younger sisters and me through hugs and fits of giggles. I remember playing euchre and canasta with her and Grandma Josephine. They were both independent, strong-willed card sharks who taught me about how to respond to God's love in prayer.

Whenever we went to visit the Felician Convent in Chicago where Paschalita lived, the nuns would delight over my two younger sisters and me, and without fail, they would ask my parents which one of us they were leaving behind to become a sister. Despite this joke, I never felt pressured by the sisters. Rather, they offered an invitation that came from a place of love. Sister Paschalita encouraged me in my studies and discernment through little prayers or words of wisdom she sent me in the mail. She was also a role model for me as a strong, female leader who had taught English to Felician sisters in Poland, worked as a teacher and school principal, and even served as mother superior. She affirmed my vocation to be a leader in the Church as few others had, and we became even closer when I started college at Loyola University Chicago.

Sadly, she became sick during my first semester, and in December, she passed away. Shortly before she passed, my parents went to visit her. With tears in her voice, my mom told me that Paschalita had told her, "Tell Elaina to take my place." I felt honored, shocked, and scared. I was honored she had called me by name to lead as she had, but I didn't want to be a nun. A few minutes after that phone call I walked to the campus chapel to pray. A part of me went to pray for my family, and a part of me went to pray about what Paschalita meant. *Was I called to be a nun?* As soon as I asked the question, I knew the answer: No.

Somewhere between that phone call with my mom and the next few years, I realized that Paschalita was not asking me to take her place at the convent. Rather, she had seen my vocation and was affirming that the spiritual strength and compassion I saw in her also resided in me. That same year I met a young Jesuit who changed my life by introducing me to the local Catholic Worker community. I encountered a new way of being church and a new way of living my faith that felt authentic to my call. Through the Catholic Worker, I experienced forms of liturgy that took place in their house, in the streets, and at protests. My whole life seemed to be shifting, even my educational focus. Through my major, I focused on world religions and spent a year doing cross-cultural research in Rome and Beijing, but the classes I took for my minor in pastoral leadership were the classes that made me feel most alive.

STRUGGLING TO FIND MY SPACE

If I couldn't be a priest, then I was going to get as close as I could. So, I still planned to do a year of service after college before applying to divinity school. After Loyola, I spent two years in the Jesuit Volunteer Corps Northwest in Ashland, Montana, working with the Northern Cheyenne and Crow tribes. I was greatly impacted by the spirituality of the Crow and Cheyenne people, especially through what I learned from my adoptive Cheyenne Grandma. As a Cheyenne elder and a Catholic woman of faith, Grandma Helen was often called on to preach at Sunday Mass and to lead traditional Cheyenne prayers and rituals. She often spoke to me about being a ceremonial woman. Being a ceremonial woman, she told me, is not just about leading prayer. It is also about loving God and all of God's creation. "You are called to be a ceremonial woman," Grandma Helen said to me. She explained that the Creator called me to share compassion with the world. Although I had always felt drawn to ordained ministry, Grandma Helen challenged me to own that vocation, to be unafraid of taking on leadership roles—to preside over liturgies, rituals, and sacraments. When I think back on my experience, I relate it to the call of Samuel in Scripture (1 Sam 3). Samuel hears God calling out to him, but he thinks it is Eli. Each time Samuel hears God calling, he replies, "Here I am" to Eli. Finally, Eli realizes that God is calling out to Samuel and tells Samuel to respond, "Speak, for your servant is listening" (1 Sam 3:10). Grandma Helen and Paschalita were both Eli to me. They helped me to hear God *and* to offer God my yes to God's calling my name.

Following my time in Montana, I spent a year as a pastoral ministry associate at a Newman Center in Michigan. As I spent time with the parish community, especially those going through RCIA, I renewed my own baptismal call to be priest, prophet, and king.[3] I was blessed to be in a space where I preached from the ambo for the first time and received training as a spiritual director. I grew into my role as priest when I ministered to students and parishioners, and I felt my prophetic identity come alive in homilies and online reflections. It was also a time when I started to come to terms with another identity. I am queer. As is common among many Catholic LGBTQ+ people, I denied that part of myself because it did not fit into the neat categories set before me by society and my faith. Somewhere between making LGBTQ+ friends and having the space and time away from school to figure out who I was, I started to talk to God about it. It turns out God loved that I was queer, and we quickly went back to arguing about why she let her church be bound by patriarchy and clericalism.

In those in-between years of Montana and Michigan, I went through phases of finding my own priestly identity by working in the confines of the Catholic Mass, finding ways to transform it, and creating my own original liturgies. I kept hearing the voice of God calling me to ordained ministry, and so I went where future ordained ministers were trained—divinity school.

As I began my MDiv at one of the theologates of the Graduate Theological Union in Berkeley, I discovered a world in which my voice and call were celebrated in one room and silenced in the next. During this time, I grappled both with my identity as a queer woman and as a woman called to ordained ministry. I once again turned to my love for liturgy but found myself more and more uncomfortable with the Catholic Mass. I felt more heavily the weight of church doctrine that denied both the sacredness of my queer identity and my call to ordination. In every space I entered, I wondered if I was truly welcome.

Fueled by the ever-increasing disparity of access, sexism, and clericalism I saw in the Church, I continued my studies. I was shocked when Jesuit classmates laughed at me when I told them I felt called to ordained ministry. I experienced raw anger when I was ironing corporals and purificators in the sacristy as part of my work-study job, and seminarians asked me if I was practicing for my future husband. When I reported this disparaging treatment from some of my seminarian classmates, faculty and administration repeatedly told me that the mockery and degradation I experienced was good preparation for what it would be like to work in the Catholic Church. I was stunned. Their response essentially condoned inappropriate behavior and challenged me. The implicit message—there is no room for me here.

I began to feel a close kinship to Dorothy Day who wrote in her autobiography,

> I loved the Church for Christ made visible. Not for itself, because it was so often a scandal to me....The Church is the Cross on which Christ was crucified; one could not separate Christ from His Cross, and one must live in a state of permanent dissatisfaction with the Church.[4]

The more I learned about the Church and the more time I spent with my seminarian peers preparing to lead it, the more dissatisfied I became.

The theologate I had hoped would be a place where I would find a new home instead became a battleground, a place where my identity as a woman, a queer woman, and a woman called to ordained ministry, was something I had to justify to people I had assumed would accept me for who I am. Feeling that I couldn't be myself in this community brought up questions I'd been grappling with for a long time. Is there room for me in the Catholic Church? Why is God leading me on a seemingly impossible journey that seems destined for heartache?

CREATING SAFE SPACES

I felt saved by the grace of God when I was introduced to a group called In Memory of Her, which created a safe space for women to claim their struggles within the Catholic Church, with special attention to the issue of experiencing a call to ordination and being unable to respond to that call within the Church. The group gathered men and women in support of church justice. It was the first space I felt truly welcome as both a woman called to priesthood and as a member of the LGBTQ+ community. In Memory of Her received its name and inspiration from the woman who anoints the feet of Jesus at Bethany: "Truly I tell you, wherever the good news is proclaimed in the whole world, what she has done will be told in remembrance of her" (Mark 14:9). The existence of such a group showed me that I am not alone in my struggles. After my first semester, I was invited to take on the role of cofacilitator along with my dear friend Luke. The group wanted to commemorate the woman who had brought them all together, and so I decided to write a liturgy for "Holy Wednesday."

I poured my heart, soul, pain, and hope into this liturgy; the prayers and ritual for the liturgy flowed through me like the waters of justice in Amos 5:24.[5] I felt the Spirit alive in my words. I found myself in tears as I wrote prayers with inclusive and overtly feminine language that had lingered in my heart for years. I felt the weight of what it means to create a liturgy for a community in need. It was challenging to write a liturgy that authentically expressed the hopes and longings of our group. We wanted a liturgy that simultaneously created space for vulnerability and expression of pain, but also offered an opportunity to encounter healing and love through an intimate ritual of anointing.

The focal points of the liturgy included a shared homily, an anointing ritual, and a communal blessing of bread that is broken and shared.

The Exodus narrative of the midwives saving the lives of Hebrew children accompanies the gospel of the woman anointing Jesus.[6] These two examples of women taking initiative serve as the focus of the shared homily, where everyone present has an opportunity to voice their reflections. After the prayers of the faithful, participants mirror the action of the gospel woman who anoints Jesus. The co-presiders then introduce the ritual anointing:

> Jesus has taught us that the call to bless and anoint is a call
> to every person. Like the woman who loved greatly we are
> called to anoint, we are called to bless. Jesus welcomes us
> to the ministry of blessing and anointing today. You are all
> invited to take a turn anointing one another. I will begin
> by anointing the first person and will then invite them to
> anoint the next person. We will anoint each other on the
> head, hands, and feet. Let us love deeply, as we encounter
> one another through this sacred gesture.

Young and old, women and men, religious and lay anointed one another. It was humbling in a new way. We were moved to see the Spirit break open heart after heart in this ritual, as oil and tears healed our pain. Holy Week became more holy because the intimacy of the liturgy brought us closer to Jesus and one another. Holy Week became more whole as we encountered one another in a small upper room and anointed the head and hands of those wounded like ourselves. We reached down to touch one another's weary feet, and we invited God to join with us. Together those gathered created a liberative, healing space for those wounded in varying ways by the Church they love.

I believe good liturgy does not depend on a presider or any one individual, and the In Memory of Her liturgy was certainly not dependent on any one person. The homily, anointing, and blessing and sharing of bread were all communal actions. Even after I left Berkeley, the liturgy continues to be celebrated. The In Memory of Her community follows the command of Jesus to enact this story "in memory of her." It lives on because it feeds those hungry for an expression of liturgy that dismantles patriarchy.

What if liturgy rooted in Jesus' example and centered on the community gathered as the Body of Christ can transform communities and offer freedom from patriarchal modes of worship? Catholic liturgy holds the tension that Jesus was God and human. He died and rose; he suffered and offered salvation. Jesus' life and death was rooted in the need for deliverance and justice for the oppressed. Jesus, the Eucharist, and liturgy serve as an anchor for liberation theologians to advocate for diverse social issues. For example, Nancy Eiesland's book *The Disabled God* contains a beautiful liberation theology highlighting the history of people with disabilities in the Church. She contends that theology can create lasting change and social justice in the world. Eiesland calls our church communities to ongoing conversion as she says, "Justice for people with disabilities requires that the theological and ritual foundations of the church be shaken. As it communes together, the church emboldens and enlivens the struggle for justice within existing church institutions and the struggle for a transformation of church and social structures."[7] For justice to reign in the liturgical life of the Church, the liturgy too must be shaken to its foundations. Jesus, the Body of Christ, who remains the Church's foundation, can be found in those pushed to the margins. The unconditional love of our Creator who came into the world through Jesus and the Holy Spirit is the foundation of the Church.

How then do Catholics shake the theological and ritual life of the Church back to its foundations and then build it back up again? From Eiesland's perspective, "the work to create ritual of bodily inclusion is vital to the church as a communion of struggle."[8] She offers liturgies that emphasize language and ritual reflective of the communities in which the liturgies take place. This is the kind of liturgy that I love, but it was not until I took two classes at the Pacific School of Religion that I finally began to have the language and theory to talk about the creative, liberative liturgy I had always longed for in my heart.

RADICALLY INCLUSIVE LITURGY

The first class I took was "Transforming Christian Theology." It was rooted in queer theology, a tradition that breaks down our preconceptions of gender, sex, and any other binary categories. For example, queer theology and queer studies in general dismantles binary categories such as male and female, good and bad, sacred and profane. Breaking down these either/or social constructs of male and female in theology is an example of "queering" theology. More specifically, we can "queer" our gendered perception of Jesus by thinking of Jesus as our mother, as the great mystic Julian of Norwich did. Mystics and queer theologians have for centuries written about the queerness of Jesus. One such theologian, Gerard Loughlin, wrote that Jesus was

> born a male, he yet gives birth to the church; dead, he yet returns to life; flesh, he becomes food....'The body of Christ is queer.' And it is in becoming part of this queer body that our own bodies—and their identities—are set upon a path of transfiguration.[9]

I realized it is not enough to be inclusive; we must also work to rewrite the oppressive language deeply rooted in our binary system of gender, sex, and vocation. Practicing the use of inclusive language that departs from the exclusive use of masculine pronouns is not always easy. Furthermore, using nonbinary language that moves beyond gendered pronouns requires effort. Inclusive and nonbinary language isn't used often enough in the Catholic tradition, and when it is used, it is often experienced as disrupting traditional Catholic language. Yet, choosing to take on the challenge of using inclusive and nonbinary language helped me to write more inclusive prayers that honored the diverse communities that make up the Church. The class invited me to queer the parts of the Catholic tradition that are both dear to my heart and those that I vehemently disagree with.

My professor inspired me to take the hunger I had to transform liturgy and actually do it. For my final project, my classmate and friend Lisa Cathelyn and I wrote a queer liturgy we hoped would create a space for those who experience marginalization within the Catholic Church. The project of creating a transformative "queer" liturgy with Lisa came from our longing to reflect the Church that needs to be, rather than the one we were experiencing in our own school community. The tensions between church doctrine and the lived experience of individuals in our school community often left little space for the authentic expression of people's individual identities. As a queer woman, I personally felt isolated and oppressed by the culture of the Catholic Church that permeated my environment, and the Catholic liturgy I experienced as a member of the community diminished my physical, emotional, and spiritual experiences. Lisa and I wrote our liturgy believing that a queer liturgy could bear witness and give voice to our experience as women, and my experience as a queer woman, by offering an alternative to the norms.

In the process of writing the liturgy, Lisa and I used queer and feminist theology to guide our choices. We started first by asking, how do we queer a liturgy for a Catholic community? How do we create a transformative liturgy that challenges people without alienating them? We challenged ourselves to find a balance between engaging tradition and queering norms. The guiding principles for our liturgy came from two questions: What does it mean to love one another and to see each person as God's Beloved? How do we attempt to find justice, harmony, and reconciliation in our church, with all its complexities and beautiful, broken people with unique identities?

The transformative, radical, unconditional love of God served as the base for all other aspects of our liturgy. All people are loved, exactly as they are, by God. Our hope was to challenge the community to see each other this way, while acknowledging the community's reality as being wounded by clericalism and harmful church teachings about women and LGBTQ+ persons. As Lisa and I prepared our queer liturgy, we did not abandon Catholic tradition, but we also did not neglect the complex realities of gender norms. Rather, we embraced the tension between tradition and the oppression that some experience because of the Catholic tradition.

Lisa and I co-presided over the liturgy and began with this invocation and collect:

> Let us begin this liturgy together, thirsting for transformation and communion, in the name of the Creator, Redeemer, and the One who Sanctifies (making the sign of the cross).

> Good evening to all who have gathered here in this sacred space. We come together with our hearts open and a desire to be transformed by the Divine's Boundless Love. As we move through this liturgy, may we trust in the Spirit, however She moves us, as we honor our identities as God's Beloved.

> Let us Pray: Holy One, we invoke your vastness, your relentless pursuit of our hearts. Gather us into this boundless love, that we can more readily recognize the faces of your followers, knowing that you welcome us fully, whoever we are in our identities. We ask this prayer through Jesus, our brother and companion. Amen."

The liturgy followed with readings of poetry[10] and John 21:15–19, which teaches us about love. In this passage, Jesus asks Simon Peter three times, "Do you love me?" After the third time Jesus questions him, Simon Peter responds, "You know everything; you know that I love you." Just as Jesus knows Peter, Jesus also knows exactly who we are, and he loves us anyway. We are asked to follow this example of Jesus, just as Peter was called to follow his beloved rabbi. This means we must truly come to know that we are loved as we are, *and* we must learn to love each member of our community as Jesus does. During this liturgy, three individuals shared short reflections on their personal experience of being loved or feeling unloved by the Church.

We then moved into the central "identity ritual" of the liturgy.[11] Our hope was to give the community an opportunity to safely and anonymously name the parts of themselves that are often unrecognized or alienated by the Church. We named who we are as individuals *and* created a space for people to realize that we are one community and one Body of Christ that must hold all these identities. As a community of faith, we are intimately connected. By embracing the fact that we are all beautifully queer in our own way, we open ourselves up to truly radical love. We are queer in that no human being fits perfectly into the binary categories or identities set before us by society. We can be masculine and feminine, we can be both introverted and extroverted, and we can be full of both faith and doubt. It is important that the Body of Christ realizes that

> we are bound together with those we like and love and those who perplex and irritate us; without all those others, we would not be us. God knits us together...because of the Trinitarian image in which God keeps making and remaking us, and likely unraveling us first to reweave us together yet again into the divine dance of unimaginable and truly radical love.[12]

Lisa and I gave these directions for the identity ritual:

We will now have a few minutes of quiet reflection. In this time, we invite you to come up and write an identity you struggle with in relation to the Church. These identities, these pieces of who we are, will be read aloud anonymously. We will ask the community present here to echo these identities. All these identities are ones held by at least one member of the Body of Christ and they are a part of our community and a part of us. Please feel free to write more than one or none at all.

Lisa and I could never have imagined the way the Spirit would work through this ritual. Members of the community came forward and wrote the identities they hold. They wrote: I am bisexual; I am a woman; I am HIV-positive; I am a feminist; I am gay; I am loud; I am a person of color. And one by one we co-presiders read these identities aloud. After each identity was read, the community responded: we are bisexual; we are women; we are HIV-positive; we are feminist; we are gay; we are loud; we are people of color. We had taken a risk and trusted in the Spirit to show up, and she most certainly did. The Spirit was coursing through my body as I saw her move and breathe in each identity we claimed as the Body of Christ. We became one.

Good liturgy is liturgy that provides us with opportunities to ask questions, take risks, and welcome vulnerability. Good liturgy is liturgy that creates the space to hold pain, love, and hope together. Good liturgy lives in the tension of our lives and transforms us with intimate love. Our queer liturgy was good liturgy. It was good because we created space for people to be loved as they are, which expands our experience of God's love for us. It was good liturgy because those gathered created intimacy through their sharing.

Lisa and I had also created an alternative bread blessing and breaking ritual to conclude the liturgy, but this portion of the liturgy was rejected by the school administration. Sadly, creating and enacting our liturgy came at a cost. Lisa and I had asked to use the school's chapel during a time set aside for lay students to lead prayer. We had a date on the calendar for several months before the liturgy was to be held. Less than a week before our scheduled date, we were told that we would not be permitted to lead this liturgy. We were told that we were making a mockery of the chapel, that we were going to confuse the people of God, that we were using the chapel as a laboratory, and that we were disrespectful. That was the first day I knew deep in my heart that I could not stay in the Catholic Church as it currently exists. A group of men, mostly ordained, had decided that what we had written was too radical. They were afraid.

In my experience of working in liturgical settings, creative liturgical experiences are often met with fear. Whenever I have gotten "too creative," I have encountered fear, not in the community, but in those who lead it. When I have fought to use inclusive language or liturgies

I have written, church leaders have told me they fear what the community will think; they fear that people will be confused; they fear they will get in trouble; and they fear being reported to the bishop. I can't help but wonder if what they really fear is change, especially change that dismantles the power structures of the patriarchal institutional church. There is a disheartening culture of fear in the Church. This fear often manifests itself in the context of liturgy where church leaders often choose antiquated harmful language and traditions rather than responding to the needs of God's people. I hunger for the kind of liturgy where the people of God truly feel the revelation and transformation of God's intimate love, and I want to experience liturgy that facilitates the expression of God's love in the whole community. This intimate reality of God's boundless love should come, not only from a priest in the context of Mass but should explode into our lives in transformative creative ways.

Here is an excerpt from the censured portion of our liturgy, our prayer over and breaking of the bread:

Blessing over Bread: I invite you all to extend your hands in a gesture of blessing: God of abundant mercy and love, we pray that you bless this bread and make it holy, that we may eat it as a sign of your love. Broken, blessed, and shared among this community of faith.

Our Creator, who art in heaven, hallowed be thy name.... Amen.

Sign of Peace: Jesus Christ, you have called us all to live in peace and harmony with one another: living not as strangers set apart but as lovers, one in unity by our love. Grant us peace this day and all days that we may always strive to be your Beloved. Let us offer one another, a sign of that love and peace. We encourage you to embrace those near to you.

Breaking of the Bread: With this bread we share a sign of Jesus' love. We are happy to be called together as a community to pray and worship in his memory.

Not only are we worthy but we are invited this evening to eat this bread. We are invited to come into fuller unity, community, and love with every person here.

We sought to enact a scandalous act: taking, breaking, and eating bread. We intended to be like Jesus who disregarded religious and cultural rules about who is allowed to join in the meal. We crafted a liturgy where everyone was literally welcomed to the table. Following the example of the gospel, we believed that we would be transformed through the simple act of table fellowship. There was no prayer of consecration, and at no point in the liturgy did we claim to be consecrating anything. We did not call on the Holy Spirit, and we made no claims about transubstantiation. Our invitation was for the people present to extend their hands over the bread to bless it, not to consecrate it. This ritual acknowledges the spiritual power of every member of the Body of Christ present by empowering and liberating them through their participation. In addition to the communal blessing of the bread, we planned to dismantle the shame associated with many of our identities by editing the prayers adapted from Scripture that says, "Lord, I am not worthy that you should enter under my roof, but only say the word and my soul shall be healed" (Matt 8:8 NAB). Instead, we led the community in praying, "Not only are we worthy but we are *invited* this evening to eat this bread. We are invited to come into fuller unity, community, and love with every person here." Through this inclusion of everyone, we had hoped to celebrate the identities of everyone present. Instead of feeling shame or guilt for who we are, we invited everyone to embrace the invitation to be a part of a loving community. This linguistic choice was inspired by Elizabeth Stuart, who writes that radical inclusion can serve as "an act of defiance against oppression."[13] Our liturgy as a whole sought to counteract the oppression against women, LGBTQ+ persons, and all the identities brought to our table of inclusion.

In the years since Lisa and I led that liturgy, I have adapted it for different groups. I created several versions for the University of San Francisco where I lived for a year as a resident minister. These included versions of the liturgy for a group of LGBTQ Catholic educators and for LGBTQ undergraduate students. More recently, I adapted it for my freshmen at a high school in San Francisco where I currently teach. Each community where I have shared this queer liturgy has met the invitation of this liturgy by courageously revealing the most vulnerable parts of themselves. The depth of sharing of the high school young women in particular stunned me. They wrote: I am not smart enough; I am black; I am Guatemalan; I am alone; I am weird. As we echoed these identities together, we responded with: we are smart enough; we are black; we are Guatemalan; we are not alone; we are weird. These students entered into a new encounter with one another and with God that day.

Creative, liberative, and transformative liturgy is essential if we want to create safe, justice-oriented spaces to worship. Over the years, I have written a number of creative liturgies that strive to find a space for vulnerability that transforms Christian theology and our world, an intimacy that not only honors the Body of Christ, but honors our unique bodies: female bodies, trans bodies, nonbinary bodies. I challenge myself to consider what it means to carve out spaces for the pain, sorrow, joy, hope, and chaos of our world. Can we imagine and create liturgy that empowers more people and offers an intimate and unconditional love to all?

LITURGY LIBERATES ME

Introducing our queer liturgy in Berkeley was a new beginning for me. It was the beginning of a new and ever-widening imagination of what liturgy could be, but it also marked the beginning of my growing sense that I could no longer stay in a church where my unique and beloved self was not fully welcome. In response to the pain I experienced in the wake of this realization, I wrote a letter to Pope Francis. While it is likely he never saw the letter, it was still important for me to write it. Here is an excerpt of my letter:

> Throughout my life, the Church has left me feeling wounded and unloved by its choice to reject my vocation....I love our church and I want to stay in it, but it is increasingly challenging to stay in a church that does not allow me to use my gifts and live my call to ordained ministry. Regardless of my woundedness and hurt, I still love the Catholic Church. I love the sacraments and I often experience God in the Eucharist. I cherish the Church, especially the Mass and the Eucharist, and I hope that one day women can take part in that sacrament as ordained ministers.

As I stepped away from the institutional Catholic Church, I sought a spiritual home. I felt unwelcome at my theology school, and I walked away with a pain that God is still tenderly trying to heal. I packed up, both literally and figuratively, and made my way over to the other side of the San Francisco Bay. I found a new home at the Ignatian Spiritual Life Center (ISLC) where, for the first time in my life, I encountered a large church community that recognized my call to priestly ministry and allowed me to practice my gifts regularly. They allowed me to preside at communion services, preach for reconciliation services and special liturgies, and even write a few original liturgies. I shared my pastoral gifts in the vast array of activities that accompany parish life. I learned how to be prophetic by listening to the prophetic voices of those around me. I was guided by the example of those who cared for others. For example, we held a twenty-four-hour peace vigil prior to the 2016 election, which opened and closed with prayer services I prepared. I also helped the parish write its own letter on the need for women deacons. I am eternally indebted to women who challenged me and invited me to ask with them, "How do we support those who find joy and life in the Catholic tradition, while simultaneously welcoming those who have been wounded or alienated by the Catholic Church?" In my two years at the ISLC, I commonly heard it referred to as "the last stop on the train out of Catholicism." This certainly resonated with me, as I ultimately found myself on that same train. During the time I called the ISLC home, the community taught me to live in that tension of finding joy in the Catholic tradition while ministering to those who felt alienated by the Church. Inhabiting this tension led me to learn what it means to love myself, love the whole world, and work for justice.

Through reflection and spiritual direction, I began to realize that through all the liturgies I had written in the past decade, I was trying to negotiate a way to stay in the Church. I tried to find ways to fit in, to feel at home, and to feel loved. I have a deep appreciation for the Catholic Church as a church that raised me steeped in ritual, but I slowly began to see that the Catholic Church was an abusive partner. For decades, the Catholic Church has verbally, emotionally, and psychologically abused me. When I was trying to make sense of my call to ordination in a Catholic seminary setting, I was mocked by my classmates who told me to go home and cry. When I confided in a professor, I was told that this experience would be good practice for the real world within the Catholic Church. I was belittled by those who refused to listen to me. However, this abuse was not only emotional, but it also became physical. I was harassed as a peer grabbed me and kissed my head, touched my hand, and once even my ankle. This behavior continued even after I asked him to stop. All of the classmates who mocked, belittled, and harassed me have gone on to be ordained since their actions against me occurred.

I was told in person and in doctrine to ignore God's call for me and to feel shame for who I am and who I love. I felt trapped in a relationship that I did not know how to leave. Then one day I met a woman who changed my life. She made me realize that I do not have to stay in my abusive relationship with the institutional church, and in fact, it was no longer a healthy or viable option for me. As I fell in love with my wife and best friend, Jessica, I felt God holding my hand and gently guiding me on a new path—a path of hope and love.

God is love, human persons were created out of love and our salvation is in realizing and responding to love. As I was falling in love with Jessica, I was also falling more deeply in love with Jesus through the help of female mystics. I came to know Mechthild of Magdeburg, a thirteenth-century German mystic. Mechthild's writing invites readers to encounter a message of love and hope that transgresses established binaries and norms. She was a feminist, queer, liberation theologian before her time who "fought against the religiously motivated misogyny of [the Church]."[14] Her work lifts up the dignity of intimate love that is both physical and spiritual and establishes herself as God's beloved. She becomes for her readers a prophetic messenger of God's intimate connection with humanity. I fell in love with her visionary writings, and her words awakened in me a desire to accept more fully the true freedom that comes from surrendering myself to God's intimate and limitless love for every aspect of my being.

In one of her visions she writes,

A fish in water does not drown.
A bird in the air does not plummet.
Gold in fire does not perish.
Rather, it gets its purity and its radiant color there.
God has created all creatures to live according to their nature.
How, then, am I to resist my nature?[15]

I refuse to resist my nature. I refuse to resist who God made me to be. I will be priest, prophet, and queen, and I will love whom I love. Jessica calls me "her priest" because that is what I am. She encourages me to preach the good news of the God who loves us and to consider ways I can create spaces that allow God's people to experience vulnerability, intimacy, and liberation. On Sundays when I preach, with Jessica sitting in the second row supporting me, I am fully alive. I am a queer, Catholic[16] woman living her baptismal call to be a prophet and priest.

I cannot go back to the Catholic Church as it is. What the Church has to offer me is not enough to counter the injustice and suffering I must endure if I want to be a part of it. For a long time, people have asked me, "Why do you stay in the Church?" People ask me this question for many different reasons. Some ask me because I have a call to ordained ministry, some ask because I'm gay, some ask because they see the Church in the news, and some because they themselves are searching for a reason to stay. My "go to" response used to be, "I stay because Jesus asks me to."

I love Jesus. He is my beloved and I am his. Jesus and I are close. Because, *and only because*, he asked me to stay in the Catholic Church, I managed to stay as long as I did. But Jesus recently told me it was okay to leave. I was on a retreat a few months ago, and while out on a walk with Jesus, he turned to me and said, "I will go with you." He did not mean that he's leaving the Catholic Church. What he meant was that it is time for me to leave the institutional Catholic Church and that he will always be with me wherever I go.

Over the last two years I have written eight new liturgies: four interfaith prayer services for peace and justice, one communion service for Catholic women, a liturgy focusing on the wisdom of women's voices or women as God's beloved, an alternative reconciliation service,[17] and a Marriage Rite for Same-Sex (Catholic) Couples. As a queer woman and a lover of liturgy and the sacraments, I needed a sacramental marriage liturgy that integrated my liturgical tradition into a marriage rite for same-sex couples that are excluded from the official Catholic Church's sacrament of marriage. Mechthild, along with Julian of Norwich, Hildegard of Bingen, and Umilta of Faenza, helped me craft the language for the marriage rite that invited Jessica and I, God, and our friends and family to bless our marriage. My hope is that this marriage rite serves all people, not only same-sex couples, by inviting transformative, covenantal, and intimate love.

The institutional church has rejected my vocation, my gifts, my identity as a queer woman, and my marriage to the woman whom God in her infinite mercy and love has called me to love. I can no longer stay in a church where my unique and beloved self is not welcome. There are wonderful places like the ISLC, In Memory of Her, schools and non-profits run by religious sisters, and LGBTQ+ spaces, but they all operate, to varying degrees, outside of the structure of the hierarchy and the institutional church. They are safe places because they are not funded or governed by the hierarchy of a corrupt patriarchal institution. These unique places have nurtured me with creative and liberative liturgy; they were able to carve out a space for me because they have created spaces outside of the hierarchical Church. They have set me free.

I dream of a day when the institutional church will accept my vocation, my marriage, and every part of who I am, but until that day, I will be elsewhere. I will be in those in-between and alternative spaces where Jesus has called me to dwell. I will be in places where inclusion reigns and liberative liturgy strives to find a new intimacy that transforms Christian theology and our world.

> God of Love, you love each of us intimately,
> And you smile upon the love of these women,
> Send us your Love that
> "overflows into all things,
> From out of the depths to above the highest stars."[18]
> Creator God, gather us into this boundless love.
> We ask this prayer in the name of Jesus, our beloved,
> Amen.

NOTES

1. Mechthild of Magdeburg, *The Flowing Light of the Godhead*, trans. Frank J. Tobin, The Classics of Western Spirituality (Mahwah, NJ: Paulist Press, 1998), 60–61.

2. Arthur Miller, *The Crucible* (New York: Dramatists Play Service, 1962), Act 2, #5.

3. During the anointing in the Catholic Rite of Baptism, people are anointed with oil as priest, prophet, and king.

4. Dorothy Day, *The Long Loneliness: The Autobiography of the Legendary Catholic Social Activist* (New York: Harper One, 1997), 149–50.

5. Amos 5:24 reads: "But let justice roll down like waters, and righteousness like an ever-flowing stream."

6. Exod 1:15–22 and Matt 26:6–13.

7. Nancy L. Eiesland, *The Disabled God: Toward a Liberatory Theology of Disability* (Nashville: Abingdon Press, 1994), 111.

8. Eiesland, *The Disabled God*, 117.

9. Gerard Loughlin, ed., *Queer Theology: Rethinking the Western Body* (Malden, MA: Wiley-Blackwell, 2007), 12.

10. We used Mary Oliver, *Wild Geese* (Gardner Books, 2004).

11. I previously wrote about this liturgy for New Ways Ministry's blog. See, Elaina Jo Polovick, "We Are Not in the Tomb, but in the Womb," New Ways Ministry, April 2, 2017, https://www.newwaysministry.org/2017/04/02/we-are-not-in-the-tomb-but-in-the-womb/.

12. Jay Emerson Johnson, *Peculiar Faith: Queer Theology for Christian Witness* (New York: Seabury Books, 2014), 157.

13. Elizabeth Stuart, *Gay and Lesbian Theologies: Repetitions with Critical Difference* (Aldershot, England: Routledge, 2003), 84.

14. Rita Perintfalvi, "Eroticism and Mysticism as a Transgression of Boundaries: The Song of Songs 5:2–8 and the Mystical Texts of Mechthild of Magdeburg." *Feminist Theology* 22, no. 3 (May 2014): 231.

15. Mechthild of Magdeburg, *The Flowing Light of the Godhead*, trans. Frank J. Tobin, The Classics of Western Spirituality (Mahwah, NJ: Paulist Press, 1998), 60–61.

16. The word *catholic* literally means "universal." I identify as part of this little "c" catholic universal religious tradition of love and inclusion of all, rather than identifying as being part of the institutional Catholic Church.

17. Elaina Jo Polovick LeGault, "New Liturgy for Catholic Women," in *Liberating Liturgies 2.0*, ed. Kate McElwee and Katie Lacz (San Francisco: Women's Ordination Conference, 2020), 79–85.

18. Francesca Maria Steele, trans., "Hildegard of Bingen: The Visions of St. Hildegarde," extracts from the *Scivias*, in *Medieval Women's Visionary Literature*, ed. Elizabeth Alvilda Petroff (New York: Oxford University Press, 1986), 158.

Chapter 8

THE MIRACLE OF SUNRISE

Offering Hope as a Hospital Chaplain

Sarah Fariash

When this group of women first met to discuss the creation of this book, I wrote a poem gathered from phrases from Dorothee Soelle's *Suffering*.[1] Written moments after a discussion centering around our experiences of sexism in the Church, it went like this:

> She restricted herself
> —the soul touched the void—
> for the answer to the words was horrible
> and clear
> "those who participate only in love
> belong to another world
> and have to expect
> a violent
> death."
> —the soul touched the void—
> This is the fate of love in the world.
> What awaits those who contradict the standard.
> But she said:
> "Tis not my nature to join in hating,

but in loving.
I will pass, then, to the world of the dead.
Mysticism will be available there also
in service of the regime in exile
solidarity through sharing the suffering."
Suffering makes people cry out 'why?!'
—the soul touched the void—
It is Christ's cry as well
If it could be answered…
But there is no reply
This whole universe is empty of finality
The soul must go on loving in the emptiness.
The soul must touch void
To love.

As I reread what I'd written then, I feel the pain and confusion I have often felt when faced with the sexism of the institutional church. I also am reminded of my time as a hospital chaplain intern and the nights I was on call. Those nights had felt something like this poem does—like a soul touching void, like love finding only death, like suffering crying out why and finding no answer except to just go on, continue moving forward.

I would lie in the tiny Murphy bed on the first floor with the pager next to my ears so that I wouldn't miss a call—as if sleep were a real possibility. My hands clutched a rosary that my grandmother had given me that her mother had given to her. Lying there I would cling to the generations that had relied on these little beads to bring peaceful sleep. Faces of patients I'd seen in the night would flash before my face and I would hold them in prayer—*Hail Mary, full of grace*. The monotony of words long memorized calmed my pain for them. For, the calls one got during the night were never particularly uplifting. They were the calls of cardiac arrest and death.

I still can hear the reverberating echo of a robot voice calling over the intercom "Code blue, Room 513, code blue." Such lack of emotion over something so emotionally startling. A heart somewhere in this building had stopped.

The first time this voice woke me I realized I had already been in wakeful sleep. My body quivered as I pulled on my clothes, and my hands shook as I pulled out my retainer and put on my badge. Chaplains come to the scene of a code blue to support family and, after the event, nurses and doctors. Usually, patients in cardiac arrest are not up to being supported by anyone other than medical professionals.

This was, perhaps, the most shocking thing to me about code blues: the violence done to the patient. To watch a hand try to pump a heart can only be described as alarming. Watching someone else's arms attempt to keep a heart doing what it's supposed to be doing on its own is not easy. The act is, by necessity, violent. There's no other word for it. Bodies are so fragile. Bones break. Chests collapse. It looks like they are killing someone instead of trying to keep them alive. That is a large part as to why I, the chaplain intern, am there. As family members wait in numb terror, it is my job to reach through the fog of their pain and fear to reassure them with a word or a touch that this is a chance to save their loved one. It sometimes feels like (and often ends up being) a lie.

Overall on these shifts in the dark of the night, the low lights of the hospital pretending to sleep, and the quality of wakeful dreaming come together to permeate the hospital with the feeling that night will probably last forever. The darkness will never end. It will always be dark, and I will always be holding these pagers that only call me to scenes of bad news and sorrow. There is only shadow and exhaustion and death. There are only robotic voices calling me to witness violent acts of desperation and traumatized family members. Perhaps I will never sleep again, but neither will I awaken from this strange nightmare. It is a strange space in which it feels possible that perhaps the Sun no longer exists and perhaps sleep is not a real thing.

So, at the end of each on-call shift, dawn truly felt like a miracle. No, it was a miracle. The fact that such nights could end and that I could go back into the light and hand off those pagers to the next person and that I could joke and laugh and go about my normal day became an incredible gift. Each night, somehow, astonishingly, came to an end. The Sun continued its slow course and light returned. I remembered that things could be beautiful, that not everybody in the hospital was dying, that in fact many people were getting better, and that lives were being saved and celebrated. It was like a kind of birth—the living new creation of a new morning coming through wounds and cries of anguish as it carved its way through the dark of its mother's body to turn pain into joy and recognition.

SUFFERING MAKES PEOPLE
CRY OUT "*WHY?!*"

When I first read Marguerite Porete, I felt something of this strange, yet beautiful, juxtaposition that seems to cry out for explanation between seemingly never-ending darkness and the shocking miracle of light. A fourteenth-century mystic, Marguerite was burned at the stake for refusing to recant or even defend what she had written in her work *The Mirror of Simple Souls*. In this book—a dialogue between Lady Love, the Simple Soul, Reason, and a host of other characters—Marguerite explores the melting of the Simple Soul into the Divine, like one "so enflamed by the furnace of the fire of Love that she has become properly fire."[2] Though such sentiments when articulated by Meister Eckhart a half century later would be accepted by the institutional church, they were rejected coming from a headstrong woman who refused to fit the model of medieval femininity.

Halfway through Marguerite's treatise on love and annihilation, the Soul comes to Lady Love—who is discovered to be God—in despair asking,

> Ah, Lady Love, but you did not tell me this when I met you for the first time. For you told me that between a lover and a beloved there is no lordship. But indeed, there is, as it seems to me, since the One has everything and the other has nothing compared to His All.[3]

THE SOUL TOUCHES THE VOID

Reading this sentence for the first time, I felt my own fears and doubts surface along with a vicious anger. I recognized that I had come face-to-face with my own question before God. I came to faith years ago full of hope and excitement and love for God, who would enact a truly new, just, and peaceful existence in a world full of death and deep injustices. Yet, I have often met in faith…disappointment. As I've tried to serve my church, I have been told, as a woman, "you can't" or "you're not allowed or supposed to" time and time again. All of it leading to the conclusion: I am not enough, I am nothing, there *is* lordship here, and you are not even worthy to be a servant.

This brings me to a memory that calls me to forget these censures. I was fourteen. I laid in bed thinking about the nature of the Infinite. Having just acquired my first boyfriend, I discovered that life still did not feel complete. Contrary to all media messages that told me that once I found a man, my story would be happily ever after, and I still felt unfulfilled. I considered that perhaps the reason for this was that our first puppy love feelings were finite. I contemplated all the things I could do that would alienate him and all that he could do that would estrange me. I sighed over how so much of our lives was conditional, dependent on circumstance and mood. This led me to try to imagine a love that wasn't conditional but that might be unconditional, that was truly infinite. This was the kind of love that I associated only with God. As I tried to stretch my understanding in this way, something shifted. In a flash, a brief moment, I could feel my soul, my heart, my mind expand to contain for one fleeting instant a feeling of being loved no matter what...no matter what...no matter what. I felt so full that I wasn't sure what I was anymore, just that I was loved and that nothing could ever change it. I was given a gift.

This gift shaped and continues to shape the course of my life. As a teenager, I began telling my friends—wracked with teen anxiety and self-loathing—that they couldn't hate themselves because I knew that they were, like myself, deeply loved and that anyone loved so much could not be loathed. Through their responses I learned that this experience I had been given was not a universal one. I began to feel that it was not only a gift but also a call. A call to love unconditionally those who didn't feel that they ever could be loved in such a way. Over time this spark would turn into a desire to serve the incarcerated, a people who are told that they are to be defined by the worst thing that they have ever done and that this thing will never leave them. They will never get to apply to a job without having to disclose it. They will never get to vote. They will have a hard time having anyone see past what it is they have done to see who they truly are. I have found my call here, in seeing the person beyond the crime.

I have often since then asked how it is that God entrusted such a gift to a fourteen-year-old. Why did God think I could hold that? Why did God think I was worthy? I certainly wouldn't trust my fourteen-year-old self with much. And yet God gave her this incredible gift, this call.

As I explored this call through more traditional and institutional means, I rubbed up against those who echoed my own doubts of my worthiness. First Timothy quoters telling me that they "permit no woman to teach or to have authority over a man" (1 Tim 2:12), and papal fans citing apostolic exhortations claim that my female body does not bear enough "natural resemblance" to Christ to properly communicate God's love to the world. And yet…there's this memory, this experience of infinite love. Even if others or even I think this vessel unworthy, God sees something worthy of gift.

I recall trying to articulate in some theology class, after having read Elizabeth Johnson's *She Who Is*, why it is important to begin using feminine imagery and pronouns to refer to God. I struggled to articulate what I meant. I knew that the inability to refer to God as "she" was intimately connected to my thoughts of my own unworthiness and to the Church's as well. However, the words came stumbling and sputtering out of my mouth:

> If we truly believe that God is beyond gender, but we only use male pronouns, then in our imaginations we limit how we can see God. To balance it out, we need to use female pronouns. Women need to see themselves in God. God is not male. We have chosen to identify God so much with the male, but that is not what God is.

And then from the corner of the room from well-meaning though perturbed lips dropped the words like ice picks into my heart: "But Jesus was a man." I could not say anything. For this fellow classmate had hit on my despair. Yes, yes, Jesus was a man. God chose to inhabit a male body. This gives the Vatican grounds to claim that *in persona Christi* excludes women from full, equal participation in the Church. It excludes women from being viewed as whole persons capable of mediating and representing the divine on earth. *In persona Christi* is a weapon used against me by "holy men." And it is excruciating. Yes. Jesus was a man and there are days I am angry at God for it and days I cannot understand it and days it makes me wish I were dead rather than a woman. When it is constantly brought up that Jesus' gender is so important to his godliness, I can't help but feel utter despair. This tells women that God can't possibly inhabit a female body. Another woman jumped in with some pithy rejoinder to his comment, but I don't remember it because his words had thrown me into such deep despair. Yes. Jesus was a man. I cannot say otherwise.

So, when my call is questioned by other people, by men, by the institution, it's easy for me to begin the internal diatribe of *I am not supposed to, I am not allowed to, I am not enough.* It's easy to let fear creep in and doubt start its march from the recesses of my brain to the forefront. I begin to cry out to God as Marguerite's *Simple Soul* does. You misled me, God! You didn't tell me there was going to be lordship, you didn't tell me that there was going to be hierarchy and pain. You told me only of love, and so of course I went toward it. Who wouldn't? I thought I would find justice and deeper love, but instead I have found this cold and lonely world where every day feels like an on-call night. I'm alone in a dark and shadowy building where I am ordered about by robotic, magisterial voices to be present at scenes of death where I cannot help, and my voice is not heard through the fog of centuries of misogyny and hierarchy. Rationally, I know I am not alone, that I have a community and people who support me, but in the "But Jesus *was* a man" moments it feels like I don't.

Even as another woman supports and defends me, it still feels like the Sun will never rise. It still feels like I am sinking into the bowels of the earth and that I will never again see light or goodness or life. I cry to God: Every time someone tells me I cannot be a minister of your love or that you could never be understood as feminine, I feel this death and I cannot see a way out. I am limited and you, O God, are limited too by this *cannot, should not, not enough.* You, too, are stuck in this male, masculine box. O, God, you did not tell me this. You told me there was no lordship, and yet it seems to me as I look around that that is all there is. I tried to choose love and have found that my fate is to die again and again with each dagger to the gut as pope after pope, bishop after bishop, once-trusted priest after once-trusted priest tells me that I could *never*, will *never* be enough to be a conduit of your love, that my female body is somehow deficient at being human, that when your book says that you came to dwell amongst **men** that **man** is all you really came to represent. I am forced to fall in line with my own poetic feminine creation:

> She restricted herself
> For the words were horrible
> and clear

Yet perhaps the answer lies in continual dying. When Marguerite confronts Lady Love with this accusation of Lordship, this is how Love responds: "O my very sweet Soul...Calm yourself. Your will suffices for your Lover. And He declares this to you through me that you might have faith in Him, and I say to you that He will love nothing without you, thus you are not without Him."[4] The Soul fears that she has nothing and that the relationship between lover and beloved is unequal, but Love reassures her that this is not so. In having given everything to Love, in having—in a sense—died, the Soul is, in turn, given everything that God has. The soul has nothing left of herself but is not without God because God, too, has given of Godself to the Soul. Both parties in this love relationship offer utterly and totally of themselves. This is indeed a kind of death. Yet, from it comes the chance to receive the other wholly and without conditions, to truly love, to truly become one.

This is not only Marguerite's sentiment. This is the attitude of Jesus. At the core of our faith is a God who empties Godself out, who shrugs off divinity and becomes one of us in order to demonstrate love and the untamed desire to be with us. This is a kind of death that results in a very real and very violent death on the cross (Phil 2:6–8). To be one in solidarity with humanity, Christ dies to Godself. It is only through this death that true communion, true touch can happen. Only in knowing death, does God know all that it is to be human. Death comes, and in this moment the divine and human touch for what feels like the first time.

Shelly Rambo says something along these lines. She challenges Jürgen Moltmann, who claims that where there is life, there is the Spirit of God. This understanding necessarily creates a dualistic understanding of death as being the absence of God. Rambo decries this, using the Holy Saturday narrative to talk about what she deems the "Middle Spirit." This is the Spirit of God present after the crucifixion and before the resurrection. It is the Spirit of God who keeps Christ and God the Parent connected even through death. She emphasizes the fragility of a God who can and does die, and she speaks of the love that remains. Rambo describes this love as "neither triumphant nor sacrificial, neither conquering nor emptying. It is love that survives a death."[5] Anyone who has felt loss knows what this is. This is the love that aches, which persists even though it now seems useless, the object being gone. It seems vestigial, and yet there it is. It remains. Rambo moves away from a vestigial understanding, however, and claims that this "Spirit is not aimless but instead is continually searching out new forms of life amid the realities of death."[6] Thus, this is not to say that one ought to run toward death or seek it out in order to have some kind of truer love. Instead, it is to acknowledge that when death comes—and it will, in any of its many forms—God is still there, showing us new paths we never could have imagined before and teaching us new ways to love. The love of God remains in and through and past death. Death is a reality and the terror it inspires is very real, but even there, God is present because through death new ways of life and love are discovered.

I WILL PASS, THEN, TO THE WORLD OF THE DEAD

The Church is sorely afraid of the death brought about by change. This is odd because we are supposedly a community of resurrection people. We ought to know better than any that only through death can new life come, metaphorical or otherwise. We must acknowledge that the Church is experiencing death now. Clerical abuses. Numbers falling. Increased secularization. Thus far, much of the Church's response has been fear and an increased grasping at power and doctrine. In spite of this, my hope, my prayer for the New Church, is that it would internalize Love's answer to Marguerite: "O Sweet Soul…your will suffices for your lover."[7] Knowing that you are loved gives such steady ground that it allows room for flow and openness to change. This love gives a knowledge of identity that allows everything else to fall away. The identity is this: we are enough for God. God loves and desires us, us alone. My prayer is that all hierarchy would dissipate in the wake of this deep heart-knowledge, which would allow a giving of ourselves to one another and to God. That we would let go of our fears and our clutched doctrines and listen to the pain and the desire of the other—the other human being with whom we share a common core and the other divine being of whose love we all have the potential to be a conduit. If we really knew love could survive change, could survive death, perhaps we would not be so afraid of death.

Mary Oliver wrote a poem called "The Uses of Sorrow (In my sleep I dreamed this poem)." It speaks to this gift: that there is newness and life even in darkness. It goes:

> Someone I loved once gave me
> a box full of darkness.
> It took me years to understand
> That this, too, was a gift.[8]

The Church is in crisis and darkness over its many scandals. I am in crisis and darkness over the roles given my gender. If only we could just turn these crises in our hands to see the point at which they transform from darkness to gift. If only we could really believe that in death, there is the chance for new life and a moment for true creativity. My challenge to the Church is Jeremiah's, as articulated by theologian Walter Brueggemann: Recognize the death here, let go, and grieve so that new life can finally begin to grow. He claims, "If God had not grieved when hearing the mocking voice of the nations, there would have been no healing."[9] So too, if we do not grieve the death of the Church, there will be no healing for us either. Only a change of heart, a death of old ways can bring about healing.

Perhaps, though, this shift is not even needed. Death happens whether we *allow* it or not. It is not within our control. Every time someone reminds me "but Jesus was a man" or I'm asked to reread the words concerning women's ordination that "there would not be this 'natural resemblance'; which must exist between Christ and his minister if the role of Christ were not taken by a man,"[10] I experience death. Each time this death of the soul takes place, the miracle is I find I am somehow still alive. The dawn comes as miracle. My own continued existence within the Church is this unexplainable, crazy, insane thing that shouldn't happen. It happens anyway. I remain. I exist as a conduit of God's love despite being told that this is impossible. So do many other women. We are the miracle of God's love and resurrection. So, I must conclude: *The soul must go on loving in the emptiness.*

Here is something I have learned through continuing to love in this emptiness. That first night on call at the hospital, I received a page calling me to the room of a man who believed that he was dying. The nurse thought he was being dramatic but respected his desire to have someone to talk to in a moment of fear. After putting down the phone, I walked sleepless through the halls and elevators of the hospital to his room. It was dark, lit only by the machines telling us this man's vitals. He looked tired, but at peace. There were no family members, only me and this man who felt death's breath whispering gently into his ear.

"I want last rites," he said.

"I'm not a priest," I responded.

"I don't care." He spoke to free me.

So, I gave him last rites. I touched his forehead and made the sign of the cross over his mind and heart. *Lord, receive this soul and care for him. You have prepared a place for him, for in your house there are many* rooms. *Walk with him through the valley of the shadow of death.* I held his hand and when we had finished praying, he said, "I feel ready now. I have made peace with all the living I brought pain to. I'm ready to be with God." I stayed with him as he fell into sleep before leaving to—at long last—find sleep myself. It was tucked away in the corner of the hospital with the anchor of my rosary beads flowing out of my hands into the sheets. His peace had brought me mine. In each other we each had found the Divine.

The next morning, he passed away. I felt sorrow and gratitude. Sorrow because this was the first person I had known to die. I had been with him just the night before and now he was gone. Yet, gratitude because through his death he had granted me the opportunity to offer a sacrament I had never thought I'd be allowed to give. He had allowed me space to be a conduit of divine love. In a moment of need when faced with death, something new had been birthed. This is the paradox of our faith and the center of my prayer for my church: that we might give birth to something new out of our own deaths.

This is a hard paradox to learn. I have spent my life learning it again and again. I do not necessarily blame the Church for not yet having perfected it. Yet, it is something we all must strive to learn again and again with each dying moment.

Years ago, during a particularly difficult winter in my undergraduate years I witnessed the first robins return to herald spring to Ohio. I was inspired to write the following:

WINTER SUNRISE

I watch a host of robins flitter across a tall bank of snow
Playing with the tips of bushes sticking up like unruly hair
From beneath a cold blanket
I'd sink to my knees out there
But they are light
And do not sink
They walk upon frozen waters by faith or by physics
And they promise me that spring is imminent,
The red balloon flash of their breast assures me
The Sun is coming once more;
Pretty promises wrapped up in bows of past experience
Yet...

It looks so cold
And the snow is deeper than past experience
But there they are
Defying what I know of snow
Dancing about as if the Sun were about to rise…

I find that my whole life has been about getting closer and closer to this odd occurrence that in death and cold and pain, life continues and joy breaks through when it seemingly should not. The Sun always keeps its promise even when it seems that perhaps it shall not, will not. So, I will join with the character of my opening poem who declares,

Tis not my nature to join in hating,
but in loving.
I will pass, then, to the world of the dead.
Mysticism will be available there also.

Pass also, to the world of the dead with me. Love will be there along with Mysticism and Middle Spirit, too. In good company, we can dance a world into being full of new creations.

NOTES

1. Dorothee Soelle, *Suffering* (Minneapolis, MN: Fortress Press, 1984).

2. Marguerite Porete, *The Mirror of Simple Souls*, Classics of Western Spirituality, trans. Ellen Babinsky (Mahwah, NJ: Paulist Press, 1993), 107.

3. Porete, *The Mirror of Simple Souls*, 112.

4. Porete, *The Mirror of Simple Souls*, 112.

5. Shelly Rambo, *Spirit and Trauma: A Theology of Remaining* (Louisville, KY: Westminster John Knox Press, 2010), 137.

6. Rambo, *Spirit and Trauma*, 140.

7. Porete, *The Mirror of Simple Souls*, 112.

8. "The Uses of Sorrow (In my sleep I dreamed this poem)," in *Thirst: Poems by Mary Oliver* (Boston: Beacon Press, 2007), used by permission of the Charlotte Sheedy Literary Agency, Inc.

9. Walter Brueggemann, *Hopeful Imagination: Prophetic Voices in Exile* (Philadelphia: Fortress Press, 1986), 41.

10. Congregation of the Doctrine of the Faith, *Inter Insigniores*, Declaration on the Question of Admission of Women to the Ministerial Priesthood, Vatican website, 1976, https://www.vatican.va/roman _curia/congregations/cfaith/documents/rc_con_cfaith_doc_19761015 _inter-insigniores_en.html.

Chapter 9

GIVING VOICE AND CREATING SPACES FOR LAYWOMEN IN THE CATHOLIC CHURCH

Sarah Kohles, OSF

"If I teach you this," said Sr. Nancy Miller, "it will change the way you pray. You will never be able to go back." It was during my attendance at daily Mass in college that I first encountered inclusive language as the Franciscan sisters edited their prayer responses to gender-neutral terms for God and humankind. While working with Sr. Nancy Miller, the director of Campus Ministry, to prepare the chapel for the next liturgical season, I requested that she, "Teach me about inclusive language." Sr. Nancy and I sat on the steps in chapel, and she addressed me in an uncharacteristically serious demeanor as she asked me, "Are you sure you want to learn this? If I teach you to use inclusive language, you will never be able to go back. You will never be able to pray the same way again. Your world will change."

I found the intensity and the integrity I witnessed among the sisters I encountered in college attractive. Whether in work or play, in prayer or seeking justice for the vulnerable, the sisters seemed thoroughly engaged and committed to what they were doing. The concept of using inclusive language in prayer was utterly new to me. The very idea that these women who were leaders within the Church felt empowered to change the words they prayed within the liturgy to honor their experiences as women fascinated and challenged me. I could not begin to articulate the freedom and grounding I sensed in them that allowed them to carve out space for themselves within their prayer. I wanted the same spiritual freedom and grounding in my own life. So, I responded to Sr. Nancy's warning and invitation to experience the Church more inclusively: "Teach me."

Sr. Nancy was right. Praying with inclusive language caused me to listen anew to the words I prayed. I began to notice that the visiting priest disregarded all the women theology majors. I also learned that a scholarship I was given because I was considering religious life would automatically go to a male student considering the priesthood, should one come forward. I remembered not being allowed to become an altar server at the parish in which I grew up because I was a girl (and even though I knew there were girl altar servers at other parishes). Each of the instances were examples of the Church automatically preferring men to women—no matter how qualified or gifted the women. There is something profoundly wrong with this picture.

Some fifteen years later, I still struggle at times to break free from the confining and nearly exclusively masculine images of God that permeate our church, in order to be able to have just enough room to breathe and pray in liturgy. As I encounter these struggles, I enjoy an abundance of wisdom figures within my congregation of sisters who point the way for me. My sisters have aided me to negotiate what it means to be in right relationship with the misuse of clerical power and have even helped me report abusive behavior. I know that I can reach out to anyone in this extensive Catholic network of sisters and will find people willing to encourage me, guide me, and sometimes challenge me in my thinking. I am blessed with a plethora of examples of living sister-saints discerning God's call in this present moment alongside the most vulnerable in today's society. I have an incredible and vast network of support because I am a Catholic sister. Through religious life, my Catholic religious tradition provides me with a profound sense of belonging and connectedness with like-minded believers who know their theology, live their spirituality, and challenge systems of oppression. I do not know what I would do without the support I have as a member of a community of sisters. As a woman in the Catholic Church, I wonder if the reason I remain is because I am a Catholic sister.

By contrast, my laywomen friends, students, and colleagues frequently struggle to find support within the Catholic Church.[1] While working on my PhD, I frequently socialized with a group of Catholic laywomen who were also in graduate theological programs. Baking cookies and cakes was my favorite coping technique for handling the intensity of my studies, and this group of women did me the great favor of assisting me by eating these treats. I invited them over to my apartment and they shared their struggles of studying theology in a Catholic seminary. One of these students came by a few times for what we dubbed "Cookies and Confession" after she shared that having a safe space to reflect aloud about her experiences felt freeing—like receiving the sacrament of reconciliation. These women became my little sisters (as I am about a decade older than most of them) and friends.

As I listened to them voice their pain, struggle to find people who could affirm their experiences in a Catholic seminary, and realize that their school institution and church were not structures of support for them, I recognized I had an incredible source of support in religious life that sustains me. That support is precisely what these women are searching for. They are gifted women, and they do create spaces for themselves—faith-sharing groups, friendships, alternative prayer spaces.[2] However, these spaces tend to be local, small-scale, and temporary. Therefore, when younger laywomen move to a new location, the life-giving faith-sharing group, the regular gatherings of women for prayer, the soul nurturing, sustaining spaces they have carved out for themselves while in school are no longer available. Moving to a new place and managing to find a parish that is nourishing—especially for women—can seem like a nearly impossible feat. I could not help but notice that these short-term spaces laywomen create for themselves contrast with the comparatively vast network of support I experience as a religious sister.

The stories of these women began to haunt me. I started to wonder how the spiritual, theological, social, professional, and even financial resources I have in abundance as a religious sister might be shared with my lay sisters. As I continued to listen, I heard these women express their uncertainty as to whether they could remain Catholic by the end of their programs. The Catholic Church is often unable to allow them to share their gifts. Without even considering the issue of ordination, these women sometimes struggle to find jobs within the Church that pay a living wage and allow them to use their gifts. Many of the ministries that their theological education trains them for are considered volunteer ministries in many parishes, which is a problem for anyone who is not independently wealthy. However, by contrast, younger sisters are Catholic women who enjoy a network of support and resources that makes it easier, even natural, for them to remain in relationship with the Church. Not only do we have the emotional, spiritual, and professional support of our own communities, but we also have ministry opportunities in Catholic institutions founded by our sisters. Besides all this, we are also connected to our sister-peers across the country with a few clicks on the internet or a phone call. This led me to wonder: can insights from younger sisters' experiences benefit, encourage, and support laywomen? What do laywomen need to create space for themselves within the Catholic Church? How might my own experiences of support in religious life be shared with my lay sisters? How might they then share their gifts and impact our church?

GIVING VOICE

Not only am I grounded in my own community, the Sisters of St. Francis of Dubuque, but I am also connected to the broader experience of religious life through Giving Voice (GV), a grassroots network of younger sisters from across the United States and beyond.[3] The mission statement is: "Giving Voice is a peer led organization that creates spaces for younger women religious to give voice to their hopes, dreams, and challenges in religious life."[4] Therefore, GV exists to create the space for younger women religious to connect with one another and to experience support in religious life. GV does not exist to accomplish a particular ministry in service to God's people or to hold meetings, or to achieve anything at all besides creating space for younger women religious. Giving Voice accomplishes this purpose by creating spaces virtually through an online Facebook group where younger sisters can discuss their experiences of religious life, connect with other younger sisters over shared experiences in religious life, and even locate younger sisters nearby. GV also offers annual retreats and conferences led by younger sisters for younger sisters, as well as the opportunity for sisters to make connections and gather locally with other sisters in their area. GV exists as a place for connection.

Although Giving Voice does not exist to achieve any particular project or purpose besides creating spaces for younger sisters, the spaces crafted by GV are incredibly fruitful and brimming with possibilities.

Because the GV sisters gather, pray together, and support one another, projects and actions organically emerge from the group as a result. A few examples of what has grown out of the gatherings and collaboration of GV sisters include the following:

- An immigration action and prayer experience that extended across the country.
- A collaborative book project that grew out of questions raised at the annual 20s and 30s retreat and led to the publication of *In Our Own Words: Religious Life in a Changing World.*
- Collective efforts toward vocation events, such as the one held in St. Louis in June 2019.
- Efforts to bridge the divide between the Council of Major Superiors of Women Religious (CMSWR) and the Leadership Conference of Women Religious (LCWR).[5]

As Giving Voice succeeds in fulfilling its mission of creating spaces for younger women religious, it also generates useful projects that contribute to religious life and beyond—even though the purpose of GV is not to initiate projects. Nurturing and protecting a space for relationships and connection creates room for creativity and the possibility to grow.

HOLDING THE SPACE

Exclamations of greetings resound throughout the Our Lady of Guadalupe monastery in Phoenix. Old friends reunite and new faces are eagerly welcomed. Laughter fills the dining area throughout mealtimes as we share funny moments unique to our experience as much younger sisters in religious life. We bring items that symbolize hope and place them in the center of our circle where we will gather for prayer throughout our 20s and 30s retreat weekend. We share our items as part of our opening prayer in the chapel. Each year we have returned to the monastery, we take a "circle picture" from the choir loft of this year's group of younger sisters gathered. The collection of annual photos of our circle reveals an ever-changing ring of women made up of those who are returning and those who are new to the circle. The very shape of the circle symbolizes the space the younger sisters create for themselves.

Giving Voice utilizes a simple organizational structure to hold the space for younger sisters, which we envision as a circle and is epitomized by the annual "circle pictures." A core team of volunteer sisters leads Giving Voice[6] and invites others to engage in leadership opportunities as well. GV has embraced "circle process,"[7] which facilitates meaningful conversations among participants and offers a simple method of organization that promotes leadership. The intentional act of forming a circle yields a participative structure with rotating leadership. There are three roles: the host, the timekeeper, and the harvester. The host of the circle conversation poses the questions that will shape the conversation. The timekeeper assists the host in protecting the space and pays attention to the need to pause, particularly if something intense had been shared. The harvester synthesizes the sharing of the circle, often in a creative format. This process allows for a shared leadership structure and promotes the idea that there is "a leader in every chair" around the circle, as people take turns exercising these roles and claiming responsibility for holding the space with intentionality. In addition, GV recruits new people to lead retreats and conferences each year. The very ethos of GV involves actively seeking opportunities to raise up new voices among our numbers. We operate out of the conviction that we are stronger when the leadership skills of everyone are celebrated and we hear from multiple voices.

The act of intentionally encouraging and recognizing the leadership of everyone invites younger sisters to view themselves as leaders. GV offers opportunities to practice leadership skills, such as planning and facilitating retreats and conferences. When younger sisters, who are often the newest and youngest members of their communities, discover that they have gifts to share with a national organization, they are affirmed in their leadership abilities. As a result, they grow more confident in exercising leadership within their own religious communities.

These experiences of connection, peer support, and celebrating the leadership of everyone, which form and strengthen younger sisters who participate in Giving Voice, lead me to wonder: What would happen if laywomen had similar opportunities? What might happen if laywomen were similarly empowered as leaders within our church?

ARTICULATING THE VISION

As part of the charism, Franciscans talk about practicing *sine proprio* in relation to material possessions. *Sine proprio* means "without

appropriating." The idea is that we do not appropriate material possessions, accolades, or positions as our own.[8] Everything is placed at
the service of others, especially those in need. This idea fits well with
the story from the early church as presented in the Acts of the Apostles
(4:34–35), where those with resources sell what they have and place
the proceeds at the feet of the apostles to be distributed according to
need.

What if women religious placed their resources at the feet of laywomen in new and creative ways? Sisters are not unfamiliar with the
idea of sharing their gifts with those in need. In fact, sisters have been
historically adept at identifying the needs of the times and responding wholeheartedly. Sisters built and shaped the Catholic hospital and
educational systems in this country. As women religious have diversi-
fied their ministries beyond health care and education after Vatican II,
they continued to look for unmet needs and responded. This may look
like protesting our government's perpetuation of torture at the School
of the Americans,[9] speaking out boldly against the death penalty,[10] or
even playing an instrumental role in passing the Affordable Care Act
by standing against the bishops who claimed that the legislation would
pay for abortions (which it did not).[11] It may involve helping immi-
grants at the border and working to end human trafficking.[12] Sisters
have long been women leaders within the Catholic Church.

The large numbers of sisters who entered religious life in the 1950s
and 1960s are aging. Even though those high numbers of sisters were
a historical anomaly, they are the "normal" of recent memory. That so-
called normal is ending, though religious life will continue, most likely
in a nimble network that facilitates collaboration and enlivens leadership (as exemplified by Giving Voice). The paradigm shift of religious
life is happening all around us right now. In the midst of this massive
transition, women religious are wrestling with question of what to do
with our resources. How do we preserve our charisms? How have we
handed on the mission to others? What will we do with our buildings?
How can we protect the land from development? I have every confidence that sisters will negotiate this unprecedented space with integrity
and with their hearts and minds fixed on the common good.

I would like to propose an additional series of questions for consideration. As sisters have been a significant source of women's leadership, how are they supporting the continued leadership of women in
the Church? When sisters left the schools and the parishes, did we leave
our lay sisters behind? Can sisters act with intentionality in enlivening

laywomen's leadership? What are the barriers that prevent laywomen from fully exercising their gifts? Can women religious help overcome these barriers? What might this look like?

If Catholic sisters have been such amazing leaders within the Catholic Church, at least in part because they are networked, what would happen if we offered similar resources to laywomen? What if the problems we are experiencing in our church today are waiting for the gifts and insights of laywomen to address them? For example, many of our brother priests in places like Iowa are stretched too thin as they attempt to respond to the pastoral needs of five or even six parishes. They become dispensers of sacraments rather than pastoral ministers. How can they really know their parishioners if they spend all their hours on the road and saying Masses? Bishops are not likely to be the source of creative solutions for this and other problems in our church, as creative, out-of-the-box thinking is not usually their *forte*. Obvious solutions, such as ordaining women, are out of our hands. But what other, thus far unimagined, solutions might emerge if laywomen were empowered as thoroughly as sisters?

SHARING THE RESOURCES, TAKING STOCK OF THE TREASURES

Women religious have an abundance of resources at their fingertips, all of which might be placed at the feet of laywomen. To be clear, women religious have certainly been sharing their gifts with laypersons, women and men, particularly associates.[13] However, I am proposing a more deliberate, concentrated type of sharing that might be useful in this time of paradigm shift. Below I attempt to take stock of some of the treasures sisters possess and imagine creative ways in which to share them:

- Sisters have the collective history of hundreds of years of experience of women structuring their lives together. They have the acquired wisdom of what works and what does not work. They have created collaborative governance structures.
  - What if there were a digital library that collected the spiritual resources developed by women religious?

Some resources may be protected by copyright. However, what about the community histories, the songs, the prayers and liturgies, the faith formation processes, the tools sisters have developed for sharing their charisms?

- ◆ What if there were workshops on collaboration that train women in building alternative structures to hierarchy? What if Giving Voice, LCWR, or other sister groups offered to be a resource in training laywomen to utilize similar methods of organization?
- Sisters have negotiated tense relationships with the hierarchical structure of the Catholic Church throughout history.[14]
  - ◆ LCWR members have shared their reflections on how they discerned their pathway forward during their recent doctrinal investigation through the book *However Long the Night*. This is a useful resource for those who struggle with the hierarchical injustices that occur in our church.
  - ◆ What if sisters made themselves available to mentor laywomen studying theology? What if laywomen were paired with local retired sisters who had exercised different theological ministries and shared stories? One learns a great deal from hearing the stories of others who have already negotiated challenging circumstances. One also heals by sharing painful stories. Creative possibilities arise in the space created through sharing. Laywomen and sisters alike may become emboldened to try new, previously unconsidered options in their own lives.
- Sisters have also developed life-giving theology and spiritual practices. They have claimed their own spiritual space by embracing inclusive language and crafting liturgies and prayers that draw on their experiences of the sacred as women.
  - ◆ No doubt many congregations of sisters have retreat centers or other ways in which they share their spiritual resources with laypersons. These retreat and spirituality centers are often heavily subsidized by the communities that founded them. What if there were

grant proposals developed that helped sisters advertise, package, and market their best spiritual practices?

- ◆ What if sisters worked together based on their
  charisms and created online resources or courses
  that enabled people to explore the variety of gifts our
  charisms offer the Church?

- • Sisters also have financial resources. Some communities are well funded and have more than they need.
  These fortunate communities will have decisions to
  make regarding their monetary resources. However, this
  particular moment in religious life is also well funded
  through foundations that support Catholic sisters.

- ◆ By contrast, laywomen do not have access to such an
  abundance of financial resources. Their possibilities
  are often limited by lack of resources, especially if
  they are just beginning their careers (ministry or otherwise). What if sisters acted as "hubs of connectivity,"[15] and assisted laywomen in making connections
  with foundations and sources of funding? Or what if
  sisters designed projects that intentionally and directly
  benefited laywomen (in whatever ways laywomen say
  they most need)?

- ◆ For example, what if sisters worked with laywomen to
  facilitate the use of grant money in order to support
  those who work with sixteen- to twenty-five-year-olds
  (youth ministers, high school teachers, catechists)
  by offering annual summer retreat opportunities for
  those who serve this age group?

- ◆ What if motherhouses offered paid internships for
  college students to share their charism on college
  campuses through Bible studies, service projects, and
  so on?

This is not an exhaustive list of possible ways that women religious
might stretch themselves to place their gifts at the feet of laywomen.
Instead, it is a sampling of options intended to encourage women religious to imagine new ways in which they might connect with younger
lay sisters for the betterment of our church.

Creating a New Circle

In order for sisters to share their resources in a more targeted way with laywomen, there needs to be a minimal level of structure that facilitates the sharing. This becomes a tricky question. Who creates the structure? What should it look like?

In some sense, this is the step laywomen will need to create for themselves. Within these pages, I am offering a suggestion of what that might look like, but this is not something that can be done *for* laywomen. However, I would like to suggest that a Giving Voice–type network, with a grassroots structure, may be of great benefit for laywomen. There would need to be a core group of initiating leaders who begin the network. These leaders would need to believe in the power of their connection and be eager to extend the circle to include more laywomen. Some key tasks for these leaders might be the following:

- Developing virtual spaces for laywomen to articulate their concerns, share ideas, and support one another.
- Adopt a minimalist structure that enables grassroots organizing. Perhaps this might include simple structures for local gatherings, faith sharing, and prayer.[16]
- Attending conferences as exhibitors in order to advertise and build the network. Key conferences might include LA Congress, Women of the Church, Call to Action.
- Spreading the word at colleges, universities, and seminaries. Educational environments offer opportunities for women to be creative and try new things with peers. Successful creative endeavors could be extended and shared across a network, expanding the impact and duration of the supportive spaces laywomen create for themselves.

Starting such a network and demonstrating that it addresses the needs of actual laywomen are important steps for the acquisition of resources.

Forming a network of laywomen could be as simple as groups of women in college and beyond connecting, creating resources for themselves, and meeting with each other. In my wilder imaginings, it could also eventually become a more formalized endeavor where groups of educational institutions founded by women create a common program in which participants would share classes with one another, meet in person at some point, and imagine new roles for themselves within our church. Perhaps part of their program would be to create jobs for themselves, leaving them free to explore, fail, and adopt creative solutions. What if their salaries for these jobs after completing the collaborative educational program were funded by women religious as part of an intentional furthering of the leadership of women in our church?

Laywomen are gifted, brilliant, and an underutilized resource within the Catholic Church. All too often they are lacking in the spiritual, theological, and financial support they need in order to fully share their gifts. I offer Giving Voice as a model of a network of support.[17] With laywomen forming networks and sisters offering to share their resources with intentionality, the space is created for new possibilities to emerge within the Church.

FOR THE CHURCH, FOR THE PEOPLE OF GOD

On the eve of the Feast of St. Francis, my little apartment was transformed and readied for a group of laywomen to join me in prayer for the evening. Dining room chairs were added to my living room to form a circle for those who would gather. There was a gray hooded robe in the center of the room, reverentially stretched out upon the floor, representing the body of Francis on the evening of his death. Plants and candles surrounded him. The space was prepared to remember the death of Francis of Assisi and celebrate his life in a liturgy called *Transitus*. The *Transitus* celebrates the transfer of the soul of the saint from this life and reminds Franciscans of their own rootedness in the spirituality of this holy man. For the *Transitus* celebration I was hosting, I used an adaptation of the *Transitus* service created and prayed by my own sisters at Briar Cliff University in Sioux City, Iowa, where I attended for my undergraduate education. The experience unfolds through enacting the parts of Lady Clare, Brother Rufino, Brother Leo, and Brother Angelo. Lady Clare of Assisi, the host, leads the guests through their memories of their beloved Francis, and the brothers share their memories. Guests are invited to read the scripted parts of the brothers. There are reflection questions and a sung refrain between each of the parts. Reflecting on the lives of Francis and Clare of Assisi led our group of women gathered to consider what it means to be in right relationship with the hierarchical structure of the Catholic Church. What does it mean to choose to stay in relationship and also claim your call? Clare provides an example of a woman who spent her entire adult life fighting with a church she loved in order to live the life she knew she was called to—the privilege of poverty. Clare clung to poverty because she wanted to be like Jesus with "nowhere to lay his head" (Luke 9:58). When she was on her deathbed, the Church granted Clare the way of life she sought. What call might women today insist is theirs, no matter the hierarchical resistance?

Together those of us gathered for *Transitus* remembered these holy figures, marked the ultimate moment of transition, from death into new life. What if this moment with these laywomen marks a moment in our church's transition? What would it mean to honor all that is sacred in our tradition and to be unafraid to celebrate what is dying because of our confidence in the new life to come? How might we acknowledge and even celebrate our painful experiences of church as events that are intimately connected with the new life to come? What if these laywomen are exactly the people who are needed for this sacred transition to occur?

NOTES

1. By some definitions, women religious are considered laywomen as well. Canonically, the Church is divided into laity and clergy. As women religious are not clergy, we are considered laity. However, for the purposes of this discussion, laywomen will be those who are not vowed religious. Even more specifically, I am primarily referring to younger laywomen who are roughly a similar age as myself.

2. See Elaina Jo Polovick LeGault's discussion of the group In Memory of Her in chapter 7.

3. Giving Voice defines "younger sisters" as those under age fifty. Giving Voice, accessed June 5, 2019, https://www.giving-voice.org/.

4. Giving Voice website, accessed June 5, 2019, https://giving-voice.org.

5. The United States is unique in having two different canonically recognized, national organizations of the leaders of women's religious' communities. The two groups have different theologies and models of leadership.

6. I served on the Core Team of Giving Voice in 2011–15.

7. Christina Baldwin and Ann Linnea, *The Circle Way: A Leader in Every Chair* (San Francisco: Berrett-Koehler Publishers, 2010).

8. Margaret Carney, OSF, and Thaddeus Horgan, SA, *The Rule and Life of the Brothers and Sisters of the Third Order Regular of St. Francis and Commentary* (Washington, DC: Franciscan Federation, 1982), 60.

9. Laurie Goldstein, "Sibling Nuns Will Go to Prison for Protesting at U.S. Military School," *New York Times*, June 24, 2001, https://www.nytimes.com/2001/06/24/us/sibling-nuns-will-go-to-prison-for-protesting-at-us-military-school.html.

10. Helen Prejean, *Dead Man Walking: The Eyewitness Account of the Death Penalty that Sparked a National Debate* (New York: Vintage, 1994).

11. Jack Jenkins, "This Catholic Nun Pushed Obamacare through Congress. Now She's Fighting to Save It," at ThinkProgress (June 30, 2017), https://thinkprogress.org/simone-campbell-health-care-663083582f55/.

12. Betsy Klein, "'They've Been Through So Much': Nun at the Center of the Humanitarian Crisis in the Rio Grande Valley Makes Migrants Feel Welcome," CNN (July 13, 2019), https://www.cnn.com/2019/07/13/politics/migrant-crisis-texas-immigration-sister-norma-rio-grande-valley/index.html. See also Talitha Kum: End Human Trafficking, https://www.talithakum.info/en/about-us/network.

13. Many communities of women religious have associates, or laypeople who are invited to share the community's charism and mission. Typically, there is a process of formation and a ritual celebrating the forming of a relationship with the community, and there are ongoing opportunities for spiritual education.

14. For a recent description of the Leadership Conference of Women Religious (LCWR) engaging the struggle with the Congregation of the Doctrine of the Faith's investigation of LCWR, see Annmarie Sanders, IHM, *However Long the Night: Making Meaning in a Time of Crisis; A Spiritual Journey of the Leadership Conference of Women Religious (LCWR)* (CreateSpace Independent Publishing Platform, 2018). This book narrates the process the LCWR underwent in order to respond to the investigation with integrity. The leaders of the LCWR share their insights and learnings as they negotiated this intense and fraught relationship.

15. Barbara Marx Hubbard challenged women religious to become "hubs of connectivity" in her address to LCWR in St. Louis, Missouri, in August 2012.

16. See Lisa Cathelyn's description of The Dinner Party organization in chapter 5 and Elaina Jo Polovick LeGault's depiction of the group In Memory of Her in chapter 7.

17. Women of the Church: A Catholic Leadership Conference meets periodically and may very well be an example of the beginning of such a network. For more information, see http://www.womenofthechurch.org/.

CONCLUSION

Sarah Kohles, OSF

It is time for laywomen to take their place of leadership within the Catholic Church. They are more than ready. They have done the hard work of looking at their lives, searching for God, and deepening their prayer lives, as demonstrated by Silvana Arevalo. Laywomen have mined the rich history of our church's history and found models of wisdom for themselves. These models of faith and wisdom have encouraged laywomen to trust their own sense of the Divine operating within their lives. Caroline Read enacts these within her life as she shares her journey of claiming her own spiritual authority. Stephanie Boccuzzi analyzes her experiences as a woman within the Church in light of her experiences as a woman in the sport of tennis and within the business world. With clear-sightedness, she reveals the limitations of patriarchy and offers advice for the personal and ministerial growth of seminarians.

Mary Perez, Lisa Cathelyn, and Kristina Ortega strive to create spaces in which people may flourish, responding to the needs they see in the world. Mary Perez challenges campus ministry departments across the country to evaluate how they welcome BIPOC students by offering a more expansive narrative of Catholic identity than FOCUS provides. In order to help all students to thrive as they deepen their faith, she surfaces the racist consequences of perpetuating a universalist narrative that demonizes "culture" as being "secular." Perez further proposes strategies for dialogue with those promoting these problematic narratives. Because of Lisa Cathelyn's personal experience of loss and grief, she is sensitized to the lack of supportive spaces within the Church to respond to the needs of young people in their grief. Lisa searched and found what she needed outside of the Church, through The Dinner Party, a secular organization that connects young people who have lost loved ones with each other. Lisa explores the intersection of the secular and the sacred and challenges any dichotomous thinking that would suggest the secular is not also a space in which people may encounter the sacred. Then Kristina Ortega provides a glimpse of her home life as she and her husband strive to raise their children within the domestic church she conscientiously creates within her home. She incarnates her faith that is integrated with justice in their family life. This is evident in her son, who decides that God is more like a mother than a father and declares that girls need to be treated fairly in the Church. Kristina highlights the rich Catholic traditions she hands down to her children, even as she hints at the need for more from the Church. In campus ministry, through engagement in secular organizations, and in their home lives, these women effectively create meaningful spaces not only for themselves but for others.

However, some women find that despite all of their attempts, they are not able to remain within the Catholic Church. For example, Elaina Jo Polovick LeGault grew up in a prayerful, Catholic home where she experienced ritual, but she felt a call to ordination. She created rituals and liturgical experiences for her grandmother's funeral, for classmates and peers, and for those who identify as LGBTQ+. Through her efforts to offer a welcoming prayer space for others, she realizes there is no room for her within the Catholic Church.

By contrast, Sarah Fariash understands her painful experiences in relation to the Catholic Church in the light of paschal mystery. She calls on the Church to fearlessly recognize that practices or teachings that are harmful to women and others need to be allowed to die. Christians have nothing to fear from death, as we are a resurrection people. She looks forward to the new life she trusts is possible within Catholicism.

Finally, Sarah Kohles, OSF, challenges women religious and lay-women to work together in order to provide support for laywomen within the Church. Sr. Sarah recognizes that she, too, struggles with the limited spaces allotted to Catholic women, though she relies on her sisters as a source of creativity, possibility, and strength. She suggests a pathway forward that supports laywomen.

Creating a large-scale network of support for laywomen automatically transforms the Catholic Church. If these women are supported, then they don't waste their energy on worrying how they will be received within the Catholic Church. Their self-assurance will increase if they know they are not alone. When these laywomen find their support and reason to stay, they will unleash their confidence and grace us all with their creativity as they fully use their gifts. The Catholic Church will automatically be transformed by the presence of networked laywomen among us.

BIBLIOGRAPHY

Baldwin, Christina, and Ann Linnea. *The Circle Way: A Leader in Every Chair*. San Francisco: Berrett-Koehler Publishers, 2010.

Briggs, David. "U.S Women at Crossroads as Gender Gap Disappears: Will Pope Francis Make a Difference?" In *The ARDA: Association of Religious Data Archives*. September 25, 2013. http://blogs.thearda.com/trend/featured/u-s-catholic-women-at-crossroads-as-gender-gap-disappears-will-pope-francis-make-a-difference/.

Brueggemann, Walter. *Hopeful Imagination: Prophetic Voices in Exile*. Philadelphia: Fortress Press, 1986.

Burke, Christine. *Freedom, Justice and Sincerity: Reflections on the Life and Spirituality of Mary Ward*. Hindmarsh: ATF Press, 2009.

Burkett, Delbert, ed. *The Blackwell Companion to Jesus*. Oxford, England: Wiley-Blackwell, 2010. http://doi.wiley.com/10.1002/9781444327946.

Carney, Margaret, and Thaddeus Horgan. *The Rule and Life of the Brothers and Sisters of the Third Order Regular of St. Francis and Commentary*. Scarborough, UK: Valley Press, 1982.

Cone, James H. *God of the Oppressed*. Maryknoll, NY: Orbis, 1997.

Congregation of the Doctrine of the Faith. *Inter Insigniores*. Declaration on the Question of Admission of Women to the Ministerial Priesthood, 1976. Accessed November 27, 2021. https://www.vatican.va/roman_curia/congregations/cfaith/documents/rc_con_cfaith_doc_19761015_inter-insigniores_en.html.

Day, Dorothy. *The Long Loneliness: The Autobiography of the Legendary Catholic Social Activist*. New York: Harper One, 1997.

Dugan, Katherine. *Millennial Missionaries: How a Group of Young Catholics Is Trying to Make Catholicism Cool*. Oxford University Press, 2019.

Eiesland, Nancy L. *The Disabled God: Toward a Liberatory Theology of Disability*. Nashville: Abingdon Press, 1994.

Ellis, Pamela. "'They Are But Women': Mary Ward, 1585–1645." In *Women, Gender and Radical Religion in Early Modern Europe*, edited by Sylvia Brown. Leiden: Koninklijke Brill NV, 2007.

Fiorenza, Elisabeth Schüssler. *In Memory of Her: A Feminist Theological Reconstruction of Christian Origins*. New York: Crossroad, 1983.

———— and Mary Collins, eds. *Women Invisible in Church and Theology*. Concilium 182. December 1, 1985.

FOCUS. "FOCUS Sends 800 Missionaries to 205 Locations to Share Evangelical Passion." July 15, 2021. Accessed November 27, 2021. https://www.focus.org/about/news-press-room/recent-press-releases/focus-sends-800-missionaries-to-205-locations-to-share-evangelistic-passion.

————. "Introduction: Transformative Discipleship." Accessed November 18, 2021. https://focusoncampus.org/content/introduction-transformative-discipleship.

————. "The Main Thing." Accessed November 18, 2021. https://www.focus.org/about/the-main-thing.

————. "The Story of Salvation." Accessed November 18, 2021. https://focusoncampus.org/content/the-story-of-salvation.

————. "A Vision for Missionary Discipleship: Wind-Build-Send." Accessed November 18, 2021. https://focusequip.org/a-vision-for-missionary-discipleship-win-build-send/.

————. "What We Do." Accessed November 18, 2021. https://www.focus.org/what-we-do/overview.

Francis, Pope. *Evangelii Gaudium*. November 24, 2013. Accessed November 19, 2021. https://www.vatican.va/content/francesco/en/apost_exhortations/documents/papa-francesco_esortazione-ap_20131124_evangelii-gaudium.html.

Geger, Barton. "What Magis Really Means and Why It Matters," *Jesuit Higher Education* 1, no. 2 (2012): 16–31. https://www.xavier.edu/jesuitresource/resources-by-theme/documents/WhatMagisReallyMeansPublishedCopy.pdf.

Giving Voice. Accessed June 5, 2019. https://www.giving-voice.org/.

Goldenberg, Lila Rice. "#NunsToo: How the Catholic Church has Worked to Silence Women Challenging Abuse," *The Washington Post*. April 17, 2019. https://www.washingtonpost.com/outlook/2019/04/17/nunstoo-how-catholic-church-has-worked-silence-women-challenging-abuse/.

Goldstein, Laurie. "Sibling Nuns Will Go to Prison for Protesting at U.S. Military School." *The New York Times*. June 24, 2001. https://www.nytimes.com/2001/06/24/us/sibling-nuns-will-go-to-prison-for-protesting-at-us-military-school.html.

Gray, Mark M., and Mary L. Gautier. "Catholic Women in the United States: Beliefs, Practices, Experiences, and Attitudes." *The Center for Applied Research in the Apostolate*, 2018.

Gutiérrez, Gustavo. *The God of Life*. Translated by Matthew J. O'Connell. Maryknoll, NY: Orbis, 2013.

Hens-Piazza, Gina. "Women: Nameless, Foreign, Misjudged, Questionable" lecture in the course Children of Sarah, Hagar, and Mary. Jesuit School of Theology of Santa Clara University, Berkeley, California, November 8, 2017.

"Herald Sun Backs Mark Knight's Cartoon on Serena Williams." *Herald Sun*. September 12, 2018. https://www.heraldsun.com.au/news/victoria/herald-sun-backs-mark-knights-cartoon-on-serena-williams/news-story/30c877e3937a510d64609d89ac521d9f.

Hill, Stephen. "My Story." Accessed November 18, 2021. https://www.focus.org/missionaries/stephen-hill.

Hubbard, Barbara Marx. Presentation. Assembly of the Leadership Conference of Women Religious, St. Louis, Missouri, August 2012.

Isherwood, Lisa. *Introducing Feminist Christologies*. The Blackwell Companion to Jesus. Oxford, England: Wiley-Blackwell, 2002.

Jenkins, Jack. "This Catholic Nun Pushed Obamacare through Congress. Now She's Fighting to Save It." *ThinkProgress*. June 30, 2017. https://thinkprogress.org/simone-campbell-health-care-663083582f55/.

Johnson, Jay Emerson. *Peculiar Faith: Queer Theology for Christian Witness*. New York: Seabury Books, 2014.

Kane, Theresa. "Welcome to Pope John Paul II." *7 October 1979, Donna Quinn Collection 5/Pope's US Visit—1979, 1 of 3, Women and Leadership Archives, Loyola University, Chicago, IL*. https://documents.alexanderstreet.com/d/1000690795.

Kerby, Lauren R. *Saving History: How White Evangelicals Tour the Nation's Capital and Redeem a Christian America (Where Religion Lives)*. University of North Carolina Press, 2020.

———— and Mary Perez. "Amy Coney Barrett and the Internal Diversity of American Catholic Women." Religious Literacy and Education. Accessed November 18, 2021. https://religiousliteracyed.hds.harvard.edu/2020/10/23/amy-coney-barrett-and-the-internal-diversity-of-american-catholic-women/.

Kelly, Benjamin, and Eliza Kelly. "Where We Serve." Accessed November 18, 2021. https://www.focus.org/missionaries/benjamin-eliza-kelly.

Kenworthy-Browne, Christina, ed. *Mary Ward (1585–1645): 'A Brief Relation,' with Autobiographical Fragments and a Selection of Letters.* Rochester, NY: The Boydell Press, 2008.

Klein, Betsy. "'They've Been Through So Much': Nun at the Center of the Humanitarian Crisis in the Rio Grande Valley Makes Migrants Feel Welcome." *CNN.* July 13, 2019. https://www.cnn.com/2019/07/13/politics/migrant-crisis-texas-immigration-sister-norma-rio-grande-valley/index.html.

LeGault, Elaina Jo Polovick. "New Liturgy for Catholic Women." In *Liberating Liturgies 2.0*, edited by Kate McElwee and Katie Lacz, 79–85. San Francisco: Women's Ordination Conference, 2020.

Loughlin, Gerard, ed. *Queer Theology: Rethinking the Western Body.* Malden, MA: Wiley-Blackwell, 2007.

Macy, Gary. *The Hidden History of Women's Ordination: Female Clergy in the Medieval West.* New York: Oxford University Press, 2008.

Martin, James. *Between Heaven and Mirth: Why Joy, Humor, and Laughter Are at the Heart of the Spiritual Life.* San Francisco: HarperOne, 2012.

Mechthild of Magdeburg. *The Flowing Light of the Godhead.* Translated by Frank J. Tobin. The Classics of Western Spirituality. Mahwah, NJ: Paulist Press, 1998.

Miller, Arthur. *The Crucible.* New York: Dramatists Play Service, 1962.

Mousseau, Juliet, and Sarah Kohles, eds. *In Our Own Words: Religious Life in a Changing World.* Collegeville, MN: Liturgical Press, 2018.

Nouwen, Henri. "Being the Beloved." Sermon at the Crystal Cathedral, 1992.

Oliver, Mary. "The Uses of Sorrow." *Thirst.* Boston: Beacon Press, 2007.

———. *Wild Geese.* n.d.: Gardner Books, 2004.

Paul VI. *Dei Verbum.* Dogmatic Constitution on Divine Revelation. November 18, 1965. Accessed November 27, 2021. https://www.vatican.va/archive/hist_councils/ii_ vatican_council/ documents/vat-ii_const_19651118_dei-verbum_en.html.

———. *Gaudium et Spes.* Pastoral Constitution on the Church in the Modern World. December 7, 1965. https://www.vatican.va/archive/hist_councils/ii_vatican_council/documents/vat-ii_const_19651207_gaudium-et-spes_en.html.

———. *Lumen Gentium.* The Dogmatic Constitution on the Church. November 21, 1964. Accessed November 27, 2021. https://www

.vatican.va/archive/hist_councils/ii_vatican_council/documents/
vat-ii_const_19641121_lumen-gentium_en.html.

————. *Nostra Aetate*. Declaration on the Relation of the Church with Non-Christian Religions. October 28, 1965. https://www.vatican .va/archive/hist_councils/ii_vatican_council/documents/vat-ii _const_19651028_nostra-aetate_en.html.

————. *Sacrosanctum Concilium*. The Constitution on the Sacred Liturgy. December 4, 1963. https://www.vatican.va/archive/hist _councils/ii_vatican_council/documents/vat-ii_const_19631204 _sacrosanctum-concilium_en.html.

Perintfalvi, Rita. "Eroticism and Mysticism as a Transgression of Boundaries: The Song of Songs 5:2–8 and the Mystical Texts of Mechthild of Magdeburg." *Feminist Theology* 22, no. 3 (May 2014).

Polovick, Elaina Jo. "We Are Not in the Tomb, but in the Womb." New Ways Ministry. April 2, 2017. https://www.newwaysministry.org/ 2017/04/02/we-are-not-in-the-tomb-but-in-the-womb/.

Porete, Marguerite. *The Mirror of Simple Souls*. Classics of Western Spirituality. Translated by Ellen Babinski. Mahwah, NJ: Paulist Press, 1993.

Prejean, Helen. *Dead Man Walking: The Eyewitness Account of the Death Penalty that Sparked a National Debate*. New York: Vintage, 1994.

Rambo, Shelly. *Spirit and Trauma: A Theology of Remaining*. Louisville, KY: Westminster John Knox Press, 2010.

Sandberg, Sheryl. *Lean In: Women, Work, and the Will to Lean*. New York: Alfred A. Knopf, 2013.

Sanders, Annmarie, ed. *However Long the Night: Making Meaning in a Time of Crisis; A Spiritual Journey of the Leadership Conference of Women Religious*. Create Space Independent Publishing Platform, 2018.

Soelle, Dorothee. *Suffering*. Minneapolis: Fortress Press, 1984.

Steele, Francesca Maria, trans. "Hildegard of Bingen: The Visions of St. Hildegarde." In *Medieval Women's Visionary Literature*, edited by Elizabeth Alvilda Petroff, 151–56. New York: Oxford University Press, 1986.

Stuart, Elizabeth. *Gay and Lesbian Theologies: Repetitions with Critical Difference*. Aldershot, England: Routledge, 2003.

Talitha Kum: End Human Trafficking. Accessed November 27, 2021. https://www.talithakum.info/.

The Dinner Party. Accessed November 18, 2021. www.thedinnerparty .org.

————. "Dinner Partier Manifesto." Accessed November 18, 2021. https://www.thedinnerparty.org/manifesto.

Verbum Dei USA. "Who We Are." Accessed November 16, 2021. https://verbumdeiusa.org/who-we-are/.

————. "Our Ministries." Accessed November 16, 2021. https://verbumdeiusa.org/our-ministries/.

Wetter, M. Immolata. *Mary Ward under the Shadow of the Inquisition.* Oxford, England: Way Books, 2006.

Women of the Church: A Catholic Leadership Forum. Accessed November 27, 2021. http://www.womenofthechurch.org/.

ABOUT THE CONTRIBUTORS

Silvana Arevalo is currently discerning religious life with the Verbum Dei Missionary Fraternity, having returned there. She completed the Master of Divinity program at the Jesuit School of Theology of Santa Clara University in 2021.

Stephanie Boccuzzi, MDiv, is Mission Leader at Trinity Health of New England, where she serves at St. Mary's Hospital in Waterbury, Connecticut, and the senior living communities of Connecticut and Massachusetts.

Lisa Cathelyn is a Catholic feminist theologian formed in Ignatian spirituality. She earned a Master of Divinity from the Jesuit School of Theology and a women's studies in religion certificate from the Graduate Theological Union. Lisa is a contributor to *Dear Joan Chittister: Conversations with Women in the Church* and serves as the Justice, Peace, and Integrity of Creation coordinator for the U.S. Federation of the Sisters of St. Joseph.

Sarah Fariash has a Master of Divinity from the Jesuit School of Theology of Santa Clara University. She has served as a hospital and prison chaplain.

Sarah Kohles, OSF, is a Sister of St. Francis of Dubuque with a PhD in biblical studies from the Graduate Theological Union. She is a coeditor and contributor to *In Our Own Words: Religious Life in a Changing World* and serves as an assistant professor of theology at Briar Cliff University.

Elaina Jo Polovick LeGault is a theology teacher with a Master of Divinity from the Jesuit School of Theology. She is a regular homilist for her local chapter of DignityUSA and serves on the adult faith formation team and vestry at St. Aidan's Episcopal Church. She is a contributor for *Liberating Liturgies 2.0*, published by Women's Ordination Conference.

Kristina Ortega has worked as an educator in Catholic high schools for twenty years. She has a Master of Arts in theological studies and a certificate in Catholic school administration from Loyola Marymount University. Outside of teaching, she is active in movement ministry (liturgical dance).

Mary Perez graduated in 2022 with a Master of Divinity from Harvard Divinity School and works at the Science Museum of Minnesota in the IDEAL (Inclusion, Diversity, Equity, Access, Leadership) Center.

Caroline Read earned her Master of Arts in theology from the Graduate Theological Union, affiliated with the Jesuit School of Theology. She is currently in the process of education and formation to work as a marriage and family therapist in Washington State.